W9-ATT-791

PRAISE FOR

WHAT IS A DOG?

"Shaw, mourning the death of a beloved canine companion, looks to the dogs of her past to understand how they added to her life. Her section on 'being the dog' in relationships is unlike anything you've read about our four-legged friends. An elegant memoir . . . A heartrending and heartwarming tale that will resonate with just about any mom out there."

—*The Washington Post*

"Chloe Shaw's voice, often lucid and funny, is, upon reflection, deeply observant and mournful, even as it celebrates what great companions her dogs have been. This is one of the most inventive memoirs of recent years, poignant and improbable as it nimbly sidesteps all the pitfalls of animal sentimentality."

—*Salon*

"In her debut memoir, Chloe Shaw guides us on an emotional journey that anyone who has ever loved and lost a dog will appreciate."   —*Book Public*

"This book is for anyone who has ever loved a dog."

—John Irving, author of *The World According to Garp*

"A beautifully written book with insights about dogs, life, and living fully."   —Lynne Cox, author of *Swimming in the Sink: An Episode of the Heart*

"*What Is a Dog?* is at once a finely observed and wrenchingly tender tribute to a spectacularly beloved and lovable dog, a penetratingly smart meditation on what dogs mean to us, and a stirring account of one woman's transformation. Chloe Shaw demonstrates how a lifetime of high-functioning efficiency in the face of pervasive if covert anxiety and a tendency to stand on the periphery of joy can nonetheless lead to a hard-won position as a fully present soul mate, mother, and writer, if we only allow ourselves to learn from those dogs who offer themselves as our shelter and uplift and gateway, and who, with their unapologetic need and effortless grace, show us how to be our best selves."   —Jim Shepard, National Book Award finalist and author of *The Book of Aron*

"In *What Is a Dog?*, Shaw deftly captures how the deepest parts of our humanity are revealed in the company of our four-legged friends."   —Lee Montgomery, award-winning author of *The Things Between Us* and contributor to *Woof!: Writers on Dogs*

"In *What Is a Dog?*, Chloe Shaw tells the story of her life—laced with loss, loneliness, and love—through the lens of her dogs' lives. . . . At every step along the way, Shaw relates more closely to her dogs than she does to other people—than she does even to herself. The quiet triumph of this deeply felt, lyrical memoir is Shaw's willingness to confront those things that scare her about being a human . . . and break through to the other side, a place where she can find her inner strength, her toughness."   —Kristin Iversen, Refinery29

"This poignant and gracefully written memoir amply embraces the complexities of the human-dog relationship in a uniquely personal way, and it's also a moving story of self-acceptance. A dog lover's warmhearted delight."　　—*Kirkus Reviews*

"Shaw debuts with a beautiful paean to dogs in this touching memoir recounting the canines who changed her life. . . . In heartbreaking, lyrical prose, she meditates on the dogs 'who shepherded me into adulthood,' motherhood, and her decade of 'hard-earned' marriage. . . . Dog lovers, take note and grab some tissues."　　—*Publishers Weekly*

"Shaw's language is lyrical and contemplative, whether relating small moments of intimacy or big feelings. This is a quiet, heartfelt, and memorable work that cuts right to the quick of the unique bond between dogs and their people. . . . 'What is a dog?' she asks. 'Maybe a dog is a second chance.' And lucky for us humans, and much like those ever-forgiving canines, we get those second chances again, and again, and again."
　　—*Booklist*

"*What Is a Dog?* is a tender memoir that showcases the vulnerable self we often risk revealing only to our pets. . . . [This] sensitive recollection of a lifetime of anxiety and curiosity will invite readers to examine their own insecurities and to find acceptance in the process."　　—*BookPage*

WHAT IS A DOG?

WHAT IS A
DOG?

A Memoir

Chloe Shaw

FLATIRON
BOOKS
NEW YORK

WHAT IS A DOG? Copyright © 2021 by Chloe Shaw. All rights reserved. Printed in the United States of America. For information, address Flatiron Books, 120 Broadway, New York, NY 10271.

www.flatironbooks.com

Photograph on page 203 courtesy of the author

Designed by Donna Sinisgalli Noetzel

The Library of Congress has cataloged the hardcover edition as follows:

Names: Shaw, Chloe, 1975– author.
Title: What is a dog? : a memoir / Chloe Shaw.
Description: First edition. | New York : Flatiron Books, 2021.
Identifiers: LCCN 2021002063 | ISBN 9781250210746 (hardcover) | ISBN 9781250210753 (ebook)
Subjects: LCSH: Dogs—Anecdotes. | Pet owners—Psychology. | Pet loss.
Classification: LCC SF422.82.S53 A3 2021 | DDC 636.70092 [B]—dc23
LC record available at https://lccn.loc.gov/2021002063

ISBN 978-1-250-78540-4 (trade paperback)

Our books may be purchased in bulk for promotional, educational, or business use. Please contact your local bookseller or the Macmillan Corporate and Premium Sales Department at 1-800-221-7945, extension 5442, or by email at MacmillanSpecialMarkets@macmillan.com.

First Flatiron Books Paperback Edition: 2022

10 9 8 7 6 5 4 3 2 1

To the dogs

This is a work of memory. This is an act of love. As such, it comes from my mind, my heart, only. Though I did confer with certain individuals on specific dates and details when necessary, the words, feelings, and interpretations—as meant with the dogs—are all my own.

May 2015

was lying on the cool black-and-white tile of our kitchen floor, resting my head on Booker's huge, hairy chest. It was late. The house was quiet. He smelled like cinnamon rolls baking in a barn. I smelled like dog.

I went to visit Booker's nook of the room often, lying along the side of his beige orthopedic mattress, which sat these days more like a hospice bed rolled into the heart of our home. At fifteen years old—your nineties if you're a dog, and a big, *big* dog at that—he had trouble walking, trouble even getting up. For two years, my husband, Matt, and I had been using a harness, which had become a part of him, warmed from the inside out like his fur, to lift him—an act that at some times took on acrobatic grace and at others reminded me of the shame my elderly grandparents showed when they started needing similar help. *It's about time to wash it again,* I was thinking, his smell now more barn than pastry. As we moved him he licked us as if to say, *That hurts,* or *Thank you,* or *It's going to be okay.* It was a glossy, bleak place at which to have arrived, but there we were every day, trying to figure out if he was ready to die and, if he was, whether we were ready to let him. *What do you know about death, dog?*

"You'll know," people told us. "Animals have their ways. He'll tell you when it's time."

As I stood in the kitchen washing the dishes at night or packing lunches in the morning, looking over at his bed amid the maze of cheap rugs we lined the slippery floor with so that he could navigate the path to his food bowl and the outside, I wondered, *Does* he *still want to be here? Somewhere down under the sleek white poof of his skull, is he scared?* These thoughts would fill up a good part of me until finally I'd cue up "The Only Thing" by Sufjan Stevens so that I could cry—sometimes in private, thinking I might upset Booker, and sometimes with my whole body on top of his. Fur, wet and matted where my face pressed in.

Explaining Booker's health to our human kids was complicated—yes, he was still with us, and yet a great big part of him was already gone. Historically, the sound of the back door opening had sent Booker leaping up and out onto the lawn. Now he didn't even flinch. His eyebrows quivered in mild recognition of the pressure change, but his body held firm to the floor. Was it his heart that had turned? Matt had the remarkable capacity to approach Booker with the same big grin no matter how Booker responded. I feel like even the dog knew my smile was pretend. Or was it *my* heart that had turned? Was this feeling proof that it had started making space for the hurt where only love had been?

Nine years. Nine years since I'd met Booker and Matt on that downy path in the woods. Nine years I'd been feeling myself walk farther away from my old, broken selves toward the woman I'd hoped might be out there. For nearly a third of my life I'd been Mom to this bucking, benevolent beast, several years even before I had human children of my own. Before kids begged me for *more* milk, *more* love, *more* "Baby Beluga," I had Booker begging me for just ten more minutes in the woods, Mom, *please*? Ten more minutes in this muddy glop? Before panicked visits to pediatricians there were late-night visits to the vet—why won't he open that eye? Use that leg? What's this lump on his head? Lying in bed at night, I couldn't quite wrap my mind around it: the dog that had brought Matt and me together was the same dog who might now be looking to us to bring him peace. How could the life that brought *me* peace be the thing in question here?

There was no baseline for canine happiness anymore. If a dog is a wolf whose heart thumps toward something human, we didn't know what the wolf *or* dog in him was telling us. What if the wolf longed to slink off into the woods and die, but the dog still felt tethered to the ache in our eyes, the way humans sometimes can't die until their loved ones hop home for a shower?

I'd cried through the entire appointment when I'd last taken Booker to Heather, our vet. I was too bewildered trying to answer her questions, too stuck in my heartsick search for clues. On which side of comfortable was he? And how far?

"Are you making your mom sad, big guy?" she asked him, reaching into her white coat pocket, the one always filled with treats. "Why would you do *that*?"

He would have wagged at her if he could have, but he hadn't been able to wag in almost two years, having lost nerve control throughout his back end. It was what I imagined it would be like to live with a person who'd lost the ability to smile. It wasn't un-common for us to help him up and get him started toward the door, only to find that he'd pooped on his bed.

"He's like a chicken," I said to Matt one morning, trying to make light.

"Yeah," he said, "except those aren't eggs."

I'd become increasingly worried about what exactly Matt was taking in. Having focused his life's work on emotional transparency and presence and *not* relying on the seductive trap of denial, this was the closest I'd seen him come to a defensive dismissal, greeting Booker on his bed at the end of the day with cheer that suggested they might just as easily set out on a five-mile run to-gether like they used to. The at-home parent from the beginning, I'd been Booker's primary caretaker for eight years, feeding him, walking him, driving him to the vet. While Matt was at work, I spent my days now buried in the nuts and bolts of canine geri-atrics. He was surely *aware* of Booker's age and limitations, but as much as I wore these things like a layer of burdensome skin, I worried about what he wasn't facing in the inevitable loss of his old beloved. It did feel like a gift my deep involvement could allow them: their time together could be solely focused not on death, but on *dog, man, friend*.

Herein lay the dilemma: In almost every way, Booker was a hearty, healthy dog. But structurally, he was like a building whose central I-beam had collapsed. There were times when he stood in one spot for long enough that his back end sank so low he looked like a sea lion or furry mermaid out on the lawn. And so what we were really wondering was whether he was happy even so—whether he'd still choose these physical discomforts in exchange for more of life with us.

I'd returned from that appointment preoccupied by what he might begin telling me. Loss of appetite. Loss of interest. Loss of lakes reflected in his eyes. But, happily, none of this was happening. He panted a lot, but it was spring—it was shifting hotter. He stranded himself in all corners of the house and yard when his feet gave out on him and he couldn't pull himself back up. But when we found him, he licked us. He made his best dog face. When he'd last jumped into his favorite lake, the one he'd jumped into for fifteen years, he'd immediately started sinking, no longer able to swim. Matt and his brother David had had to jump in and rescue him. But was it fair to say that he seemed happy for having tried? Within the panic was there still the exquisite, cool smell of the lake?

Finally, though, came the day when the panting's origin seemed to be not heat but preoccupation, misery maybe. It wasn't *that* hot. Our other dog, Safari, wasn't panting. Like that—and without hesitation—I knew. Whether or not he was telling me, I had come to the place where *I* was ready. As his human, I knew more than he did. I knew the way to make it all better.

When Matt came home, I tried to speak but cried instead.

"I think it's time," I finally got out.

He cried so quickly I knew he thought so, too.

I emailed Heather and asked all kinds of questions. Would she come to the house? How does it work? What would it look like? What do we do with Safari, whose lifeline for seven years had been this magnificent dog? We felt lucky. She *would* come to us. She would give him a sedative first so that he would fall asleep, then she would deliver the lethal injection. It could look like a lot of things, but most often, it was peaceful. Safari shouldn't be there for the procedure, but we should let him visit Booker's body once he was gone. Animals have their own way of acknowledging death and their bond was so great there was worry Safari might otherwise spend the rest of his life searching for his friend. But we should be prepared for anything. Safari might lie on top of him and refuse to get up. He might hump him. He might have no interest in him at all.

We set a date. Saturday, June 20. My parents, who live nearby, would take my kids for the overnight before to give Matt and Booker and Safari and me some time for our love, space for our sorrow. For a few weeks, Matt and I talked more and more with our son, Jackson, five, and our daughter, Rae, two, about how Booker wasn't doing so well, he wasn't as happy anymore, he was starting to fade. We didn't say *sick*, because what if they or we got sick? We tried to keep it vague but truthful and not scary. Before I could acknowledge the scope of what was happening, I was standing at the smoldering, bright epicenter of death—the planning for it, the anticipation of it, all the gold, gritty details that come to define the echo-shaped absence of life—and I'd never done death before. Which is not to say I'd never loved anyone who'd died. I'd just always kept those deaths, those uncontainable losses, at an arm's length, or a heart's length, so as to feel them less. As much as I could, I'd looked the other way. Not this time. This time was different.

My children didn't know it, but Booker was the first dog of my adult life. He was the dog part of the marriage that had patiently discovered in me a human I had yet to know, the one I'd been hiding from ever since I first learned about dogs—and with them, the immediate, if unsustainable, interpretation that a dog is a fine cocoon in which a human can grow. Though it would take years to see it, it wasn't until I had Booker as my steady witness, my driving muscle of dog love, that I started to surrender to the frightening but worthwhile world of human love. He accompanied me in being *me* when I'd always thought that being the dog was enough. So his death, like his life, was not only gigantic—it was the first time I'd experienced the dog from the outside, as part of the vital forces encouraging me to separate and grow. Out of gratitude *and* despair, I made Booker's death my full-time job. There was no alternative, mind or body. Soon I would have blisters from spending the week digging a grave for him with Matt.

"I just hope he doesn't die," my son said one afternoon.

I was relieved he'd said the word first and I didn't have to.

"Well, he's going to die," I said. "We just don't know when."

"Yeah, because everyone dies," he said.

"That's true," I said.

"When do you think I'll die?" he asked me.

I didn't tell him that he'd already died a million times in my head.

"Not for a long, long time," I said.

"Do you think I'll die before you?"

"I don't think so, love."

"I think Moma's going to die before both of us because her hair is the whitest."

Moma is what he calls my mother.

"Well, she's also older than we are, so that would make sense, but I don't think she's going to die anytime soon either. I think we're all going to have a lot more fun together."

"Yeah," he said, but he had Jupiter Eyes, as he called them. They were far-off.

That afternoon, my daughter, who called Booker "Buh-ber,"

pulled her tiny red rocking chair from the living room into the kitchen, right up next to Booker's bed. She didn't say anything. She just rocked, pushing her foot into the corner of his bed.

It was the night before The Day, and Matt had moved Booker's bed into the living room. It was hot. Matt was sweaty from having just finished digging the great hole into which, the next day, soon after eleven, Booker would go. During my last digging shift, it had occurred to me that his grave was the size of a child's and that he was our baby, after all.

Matt opened a beer, got down on the floor with his friend of fifteen elemental years, and turned on *Game of Thrones*. I have a picture of them sitting there, from behind. For that one moment, they were back to their essentials, the way they were before I met them, man and beast, getting each other through another day of it. Matt periodically wept as Booker seemed to vacillate between vast gratitude and panting discomfort.

Afterward, Matt brought Booker and me outside and took some pictures of us in the fading light, since I'm the one always taking pictures. If dogs have their one person, Matt was certainly Booker's, but I think I was a close second. Actually, I think you could say that I was Booker's mama, complete with rules and regulations and ferocious, bone-crushing love. Matt was Booker's one true friend—the one who snuck him leftovers when Mama's back was turned.

The night ended quietly with lingering kisses to Booker's still-warm head. I looked at Safari as I went up for the night. He couldn't know what was to come, could he? *We're going to be okay*, I told him, but I was crying. What did he make of crying?

Of butterflies? Stone walls? Dancing? God? Memory? Sex? Death? In Amy Gerstler's poem "The New Dog," the new dog wonders, "Who's the ghost in the universe behind its existence, necessary to everything that happens? Is it the pajama–clad man offering a strip of bacon in his frightening hand (who'll take me to the park to play ball if he ever gets dressed)? Is it his quiet, wet-eyed, egg-frying wife? Dear Lord, is it me?"

I pictured the two of them spending the night together on Booker's bed—Booker, preparing for death, and so, preparing Safari for life.

Here's how you fly, my friend. You get your running start just outside the cottage door and you run batshit down the path, listening for them to say, Car! Car! but if they don't, you just keep fucking going. Slow down when you hit the top of the stairs on the other side of the road. If you don't, you'll make an ass of yourself going tail-over-head all the way down to the water, which I've never done, but the close calls stay with you. You could tear a leg, and I've torn two legs, and you don't want surgery no matter how nice they are to you in your shrunken cone-hole of a world after. So, like I said, you're doing a careful Steph Curry quick-step down the stairs, which will feel funny, but funny is a human thing. Remember that. Either way, just get yourself there, to the hot, splintery landing of the dock. Don't be distracted by the little stone beach with the dead fish on it. There's time for dead fish later. Now is the time to run. If you stay the course on the wood to the right, you'll have a sharp left turn to make onto the dock. Maybe try to use your tail the way cheetahs do, like a rudder. As you should on the stairs, keep a sane rate of speed here, but don't look like you've gone soft, like you're not still the fastest fucking canine that's ever come down the runway. Which you aren't, of course. I am. But, hey, you go, Dog. You're almost there. Be the rocket. Dig deep. Sink those fucking claws in. Your only job here is to run, run

like the squirrels when they hear Her let us out at dawn, though straighter.
You're almost at the end, and when you get to the end, you're going to
lift off and jump all at once. Does that make sense? You want to get up
as high and out as far as you can. Ready? One, two, three . . .

The morning was endless. Matt and I paced about the house, as if movement would bring the hour of eleven closer, sooner, but also, maybe, push it all the way back to never. Though I couldn't yet fathom what we had to survive to get there, and though we certainly weren't ready to be *without* him, we were ready to be on the other side of this. We were ready for him to be peaceful.

After it dawned on me quite suddenly that I'd put no thought into what would suffice as his last meal, I rummaged through the refrigerator and came out with two hot dogs. Momentarily racked with guilt that I hadn't prepared a stuffed goose or filet mignon, I decided this was Fun Mom's answer to a life spent saying no to table scraps. The last great gift of junk. (Though I'm not sure hot dogs *aren't* filet mignon to a dog.)

Heather and her vet tech, Lori, arrived. My stomach tingled in the excited way it had that first day I met Man and Dog, but with a terrible dread shot through. I'd never hugged Heather or Lori before, but that's how we began. If vets have their secret favorites, Booker was one of Heather's. The sound of her voice usually made him bounce, but not today. Today he waited for her to join him on the floor. I took a picture of them there together.

Heather and Matt walked Booker out to the back of our yard, where we'd laid the big blanket we'd wrap him in. I made sure

Safari was inside, then followed in the narrow path of everything right before me. There was no broad, bird's-eye view of this. It was too big. There was only the muffled immediacy of being inside it. I was light. I was leaves. I was human. I was air.

I arrived under the crabapple tree given to us by our dear friend Dee when we moved here. Dee was one of Booker's favorites, so it felt good that she was somehow here with us—with him—too. Booker was on the ground, so we got on the ground with him. He was panting hard. He must have known this backyard gathering was unusual. The vet belonged in the vet place, not *here*. I held his paw. Matt scratched him the way he always did, behind the ears.

Matt and I cried from beginning to end. We watched him, kissed him, held him, as his panting slowed and he gently lowered his head. That head had bones in it you could cut stone with. That head got so hot by the summer lakes. I remember realizing as he finally closed his eyes that I'd never see them again. Those enormous brown eyes filled with goop and sun. When his heart stopped, he was on his side with his front paws arced up under his chin like he was midleap from wherever he had been to wherever he meant to go.

I didn't think he'd look much different once he was dead, but he did. I'd never seen anything so still. He looked like a picture, like he was already a portrait memorialized on our wall. All the leaps those legs took—up a ledge in the forest, off our back porch, out into the cold blue ripples of Keuka Lake. I hoped to God, if there was a God, as he lay there that that was what was playing for him against the pink-to-gray insides of his lids.

I leaned in for a last kiss where I've kissed every beast I've ever loved—right between the eyes, where what I've always called the Wild Eye is. It was so hard to pull away from the only thing I'd ever watched die, the only beating thing I'd ever watched stop.

Then Matt let Safari out. We all stood back to give him room. When you live with dogs, you learn their patterns. They famously thrive on a schedule. They find comfort in routine. But when you live among dogs you must also be ready for the *dog* in the dog to step out and surprise.

Wagging softly, Safari walked right up to Booker's face. Their noses touched. Then Safari backed away and came over to us. We gave him a few supportive scratches. He trotted a large circle around Booker's body, returning once more to the place he'd licked a billion times, the place he'd looked to most those seven years they'd had together for direction, companionship, faith—Booker's face. Their noses touched like strawberries on a shared stem. I wondered if what he was doing was similar to what I've heard grief looks like in the world of wild horses, that they gather to breathe deep, hot breaths over the dying horse's muzzle. Then Safari trotted back to us. He seemed neither anxious nor distraught. I thought this moment would break him, because I thought it would break me. He wagged the low wag of acknowledgment, perhaps. He seemed to understand. The only unusual behavior he exhibited was that for the first time ever, he spent the entire afternoon on Booker's bed.

If only we humans were so lucky as to mourn with such brazen immediacy. We so often instead hide our broken hearts in shame; a dog *becomes* the broken heart.

We hugged Heather and Lori again, wrapped Booker in the moving blanket, and lowered him down. When the kids got

home, we would find rocks to paint and place over the spot
where Booker now lay.

A few hours later, my parents pulled up and chattily, busily got
the kids and the kids' things out of the car so they could leave
quickly and avoid crying themselves. Right there on our back
porch, where so often we'd sat with the dogs, watching the
hummingbirds zip through summer, we told Jackson and Rae
that while they were at Moma and Pa's, Booker had died. At two,
Rae knew the right face to make but not the corresponding
emotion. Jackson immediately announced that he was fine.

"It's okay to be sad," we told him. "We are *so* sad."

"I'm not sad at all," he said.

But after a pretty splendid tantrum, I got him in my arms
and hugged him until he collapsed into me with a sobbing-mad
sadness. That night, we *all* slept as if we had rocks on top of us.

I woke the next morning too dark and early, too crippled by
what was real, what was lost, what remained, and, no matter the
answers, by life's savage demand that we keep moving forward
anyway.

The Dog House

've begun thinking too early again and now I'm up for the day, before the dogs even, the dark woods behind the house lighting up in small patches, the sun trickling through, as if cued inside a theater. The fuzzy rays stretch to reach between each plant and tree like the spindled haze of a spell. First the low ones—the ferns and moss and prickly thickets—then each tree lights up for its own dramatic monologue, most towering high above the white begonias the kids and I planted around Booker's grave to mark the first anniversary of his death.

The Dog House is the name I've given our family home for my one week alone with the animals. Despite the eighties sitcom references that might come to mind, I've done nothing wrong to land here. In fact, being in *this* Dog House is a treasure. My cats, Tito and Lolita; my dogs, Safari and Otter; and me. The kind of alone that is perfect. The kind of alone where I can be less human for a while, more beast. This cockeyed human-to-animal ratio is where I've learned to be most reliably *me*. Or, at least, I've always believed so.

Our yellow colonial just outside New Haven sits up on a

small hill over a pretty busy country road, though our life orients out back, where a couple of grassy acres meets a wild stretch of brook and woods. Built in 1759, it was one of the first houses in the area. It has the expansive, buckled floorboards; cupboards of warped old glass; and cooking hook in the fireplace to prove it. An arborist who visited to assess the trees not long after we moved in determined that some of them likely date from around that time, too. Sugar maples, three Japanese maples, and one giant catalpa that grows its leaves out slowly all summer until they're elephant ears. Since we moved here in 2012, I've watched these trees in all kinds of storms, leaning into the weather, not away from it, the way skyscrapers are built to move ever so slightly in order not to fall. I have watched them do what trees do with the same quiet reverence with which I watched the buildings of New York City as a child. For eighteen years, from the benches on the Brooklyn Heights Promenade, I watched Manhattan, that dazzling crocodile, as it lit up and aged with me, my architect father's own neon thumbprint pulsing all over the city. Dad: preserver of old giants, raiser-up of new ones. But these trees are my skyline now. They've dropped baby squirrels and raccoons on us when their mothers went missing, as if to say, *Your turn to mother the wild.*

It's been more than a decade (a decade of marriage and childbearing) since I've experienced this kind of solitude—a decade since I've considered the meaning of Me without the perpetual presence of Other. Who am I without my mother and father? My husband and children? My family and friends? The treasured dog who shepherded me into adulthood with the unassuming grace only an animal can muster? And *why* am I? The answers, I hope, are waiting for me somewhere inside the days to come and the abiding, essential blankness of Alone. Yet who knows how I'll find them, locate the source of a life that has been so filled and now overwhelmed with anxiety it's hard to sleep, hard to be still, hard now to be even where I've always felt safest, among the soft, oystered muzzles of dogs.

One year has passed since Booker died, and I'm only now stopping long enough to consider all that dog and death did to me—and for me. What life, so far, has done. What I have, or have not, done in response. It's the first time, for my humans, for *me*, I've felt willing to try to shed the part of me that's always *gone dog* instead of fully embodying the human. *What is a dog? What is a human? What is the meaning of one without the other?*

Yet this solo mission means missing our family summer vacation—I won't get to see what tiny and giant leaps the kids might make on the lake this year; I won't get to live out this huge little part of their lives with them. So it's with a heavy, pounding fist in my throat that I choose Me over Them for a week. While I don't want to miss a second with them, I feel I've already missed too many years with me.

Sometime deep and dark in my first night, I wake to find that the house isn't human *or* dog, but something else entirely: it's the three a.m. house in my head. I've had many houses in my head over the years. There was the house where my *real* parents lived—not the ones I called Mom and Dad, who played the part so dutifully, but the long-lost ones to whom I was convinced I must have once belonged, ones who had to feel and be more like me. There was my fantasy house, designed at my dad's drafting table, for my future self: a farm full of horses on one side and an ocean full of whales on the other. And there was the three a.m. house, the most dreaded house of all. Never loving or cozy, this house fills with horror at the precise hour when my mind most often gets away from me, and away it goes. From my bed, I carry out the exercise astronaut Chris Hadfield practices when pre-visualizing his next stint in space. *What's the worst thing that can happen?* he asks himself, before proceeding step by step through the possibilities, patiently orchestrating fixes. I lie wide awake alone at the hour of owls, blinking like one, or *not* blinking like one, but without the invigorating rodent appetite to keep me company. But I'm not an owl—or an astronaut—and have the sour stomach of wanting nothing but to sleep. I'm lit up with the dark part of solitude that's always plagued me—the terrifying feeling that there is nothing holding me but me. I've asked for this solitude, craved it even—how else in a house full of humans to find the space to think?—but now I want nothing more than to feel the oxytocin overload brought on by my husband's radiant body when I reach out my hand. I want my daughter to appear bedside, crazy haired, mid-dream, and ask to climb in. I want my son to do the same.

It is Safari who smells my *ache* and *awake* and periodically does a whimpering lap around the bed. I always feel that everything is okay if the animals are acting normal, and this soft whimpering is normal for Safari. Even when he's nervous, he doesn't look unhappy, being somewhat paradoxically fitted with a dolphin's perma-grin. If I speak to him, he wags, whimpers more. He walks over and gives me his whole head in my hands, making eye contact so hard it feels primitive, like we're the first human and wolf to meet.

There's a theory that the first wolves to more closely connect with humans happened to be, on the great scale of wolf etiquette, nicer wolves than average. At least for the moment, the nicest wolf of all is holding me the best way he can, pulling me out of myself enough for me to see that I am scared but nothing scary is happening; I'm scared but surviving; I'm scared but have a decade of hard-earned marriage and motherhood to remind me that I'm not only scared—I might be brave, too. If I could only feel it.

At around ten a.m., I'm sitting at my desk, reading in the company of the dogs around my feet and the family photos on the wall, when there's an explosion outside. Something very big in my right peripheral vision comes down. In an instant, Otter and I are paws-up at the window, while Safari lies low under my legs. A car has driven off the road and taken down an entire electrical pole in the exact spot where the dogs and I stand every day while we wait for a clearing in the traffic to cross back over after walks. The pole's thick, split self and the great spiderweb of its nearly twenty wires, some sparking, cover the road. Head-to-toe shaking, waiting for signs of life, I dial 911. The driver's-side door opens a little, but it's too wedged in by the foliage. A few seconds later, the passenger-side door opens and someone, a young man I would put around twenty, falls out. He's standing now, feeling his body, doubling over, shaking his head around as if to wake up, catch up, take it all in, or *try*, the marshmallow of air bag poofing out behind him. He walks into the middle of the road.

Cars start to gather—a few police and a fire truck. They make Otter howl a deep, authentic, wild howl. He always does this when sirens pass. While he's still up near the window with me,

Safari stays low, preferring not to look too directly at the things that scare him, the things that move too much or make too much noise, the way I've always watched scary movies without sound. In contrast, Otter wants to be at the center of whatever's moving *most*. On a normal day, Otter's heart spikes into excitement mode at the drop of a hat (*Wind! Flashlight! Dish towels!*), so he seems almost baffled at the real-life emergency here. He and Safari both stay with me, keep a pack with me, following me so close, they're petticoats. If Booker were alive, he'd be all in, too.

A fireman comes up the driveway, so I open the front door.

"Power out?" he asks when I step out.

"Yep," I say.

I'd put him in his late fifties.

"You're going to want to turn your main breaker off so there's no power surge when it all comes back on later. You know where to find it?"

I'm trying to look like I'm having intricate, electrical-themed thoughts, but I don't know where the main breaker is, so all I'm doing is picturing us in the basement in the dark together. I give myself a quick, internal pep talk, trying my hardest to trust the humanity here over the calamitous worst-case scenarios always playing in my head. The fact that there is such a thing as bad guys means that there are good guys, too. The fact that there is grief means there's love. My friend Larry taught me that. "I'm okay being the Grief Guy," he told me a few years after his wife died. "Because that means I also get to be the Love Guy." So, armed with the Love Guy, the Good Guy and I make our way down into my 1759 basement, in which the house's original owner is rumored to have locked his daughter so she couldn't get married—but not before the Good Guy thoughtfully suggests he let the barking dogs sniff him out, meet him, before entering *their home.* His words. Clearly the Good Guy is also a Dog Guy.

"*Easy,*" he says to Otter, who's a bit of an excited hopper. *Easy, Easy,* I hear my babysitter Burke telling my first dog, Easy, when she'd jump up on him.

"Who's this?" he asks.

"Booker," I say. "Sorry, *Otter,*" I add, correcting myself. "Booker was our old dog. He died a year ago. I guess I still don't believe it."

"We lost our dog Shep five years ago," he said. "And still haven't been able to replace him. They break your heart. You're a good dog." He scratches under Otter's chin.

I didn't expect to be followed by this grief for so long, but here I am, here it is in its most stubborn, perplexing form. It's as if, the way some people feel phantom limbs after losing an arm or leg, I'm never without my phantom dogs. We have Otter now, but were we ready for him? Does he sense around him a persistent sorrow? Where in a body does grief you dare not speak of go? It feels as if in Booker's absence I've *become* Booker, absorbed him like an octopus covers its prey. The conundrum of which is partly why I am here. I can't be Booker anymore. My family needs me to be *me.*

I walk to the end of my driveway. It's brutally hot, in the nineties today. Men in different uniforms are walking this way and that. One of the men from the electrical company passes by and asks, "What happened here, anyway?" He has arrived to do his job and he doesn't know why, other than the obvious: there's a mess to clean up, a pole to replace, wires to be restored. He doesn't know the *story.* "That's why when there's an earthquake the helpers come from afar," my friend Megan later points out. It gives me goose bumps.

We spend the day watching men work, watching each other watch men work, watching systems of physics, watching all of these humans, because of one man, collide. They did their jobs and went home to stories—and maybe dogs—of their own, where they're *allowed* to know the stories, where they can be remembered and loved, the way I am in my own home. We thought we watched a young man die. But what we watched was a young man survive. *Does his survival mean my survival, Dog?*

In a world of chaos and confusion, what an anomaly of the rational and humane. In my house, today, it looked like this: the dogs maintained the pack so that I could hold the story, keep space for the witness now in me; I held the story so the helpers could help. And it worked.

While I'm reading in bed that night, Safari reappears. He makes his little whimper and licks my face. Then he gives me the Eyes, the ones that make me believe he's capable of talking but just hasn't done it yet. These eyes tell me so much. But *what*? What do dogs make of solitude? Electrical poles? Trauma? I'll never know. Why do I avoid the science of dogs? People send me books, links, articles. I almost never read them. What *don't* I want to know about the dogs I know? Isn't it enough to know that a dog is the mad rapture of something beloved?

"Wanna come up?" I finally say, patting the bed.

He hops up and lies on top of me the way my childhood dog Agatha used to before moving down to sleep on my feet. He's never done this before. Not only is he not allowed on the bed, if he's ever snuck up, it's never been for long. And he normally likes touching hands and faces but not entire bodies.

Booker? Are you here?

"Hey, bud," I say, holding him. "What a way to start the week, huh?"

He just lies there for a few minutes. His need pulls me out of my need into the shared space of enduring the next thing, and the thing after. He curls in like a kid curls in, letting me care for him this way while my human kids are gone.

I sleep like a whole cave of flipped bats. Maybe it's because I'm that tired, maybe it's because my close proximity today to something so infused with fear shook the fear right out, maybe because I'm finally letting go a little, making space for the possibility that there really is a system at work, a more intimate kind of help system, that's been, dog by dog, showing itself, holding me.

Easy: Dog of Siblinghood

(1975–1979)

What is a dog? In the cosmic burnout of my bright, briny beginning, I didn't yet know the answer to that question, same as I didn't know the answer to: What is grief? What is a hummingbird? What is love? As I imagine it, eventually my mother or father must have pointed to our old Afghan hound, Easy, and said, "Dog." Okay, I must have thought. I see the dog, but what *is* it? I see its eyes, its nose, its tail trailing hair like tentacles. But what is a tentacle? *What is a dog?*

My parents were newlyweds when they got her from a breeder, who, in addition to selling Egyptian puppies, was an organizer in the activist group Students for a Democratic Society in New Haven, Connecticut, where my parents lived while my dad attended architecture school. They'd been given a black cocker spaniel puppy named Clyde as a wedding gift, and they thought Clyde needed a friend—though eventually, Clyde would go to live in Texas with my dad's aunt, who was lonely and grieving after her own dog had died. My mom had had Afghans on the brain ever since seeing them all over the Upper East Side when she was a student at Barnard. Easy was officially named Ysé, a name my mom, the French major, found in French literature. That is where she also found the name Chloe, the Greek goddess of fertility, though I was nearly named Electra since my maiden name, Bland, seemed to beg for something a little electric. (I spent more than a few hours in my thirty-three years as Chloe Bland wondering who Electra Bland would have been—and from time to time I even tried to channel her, believing Electra capable of all the things Chloe wasn't.)

Easy's ancestral Egyptian name was Abaicor. But, in a rational nod toward our non-French, non-Egyptian heritage, she became good old American Easy. And good old American Easy followed my parents from New Haven, to Brooklyn, to Miami (where I was born), then back to Brooklyn for good.

Easy was my parents' first baby—even in the way she first greeted me, their second baby, when they brought me home to Coconut Grove. My dad loves to describe how they presented her with this warm, swaddled-up, black-haired thing that was me. She took one sniff, lowered her head, and, like a demoted Disney dog, slinked back to her spot on the floor.

I wonder if she ever got over that feeling or if it just became part of her along with everything else to which wolves who've *gone dog* must adjust: stairs, crowded apartments, fire trucks. I was quite young and so don't remember life with Easy particularly well, though somehow her sheer size suggests to me that I should.

I do, however, remember bits and pieces—her silky yellow hair, for one. I remember how she used to jump up on my babysitter, Burke, like a giant praying mantis wearing a blond wig. "*Easy*, Easy," he loved to say. I remember our cat, Pearl—who'd quickly and understandably developed a distaste for me when

I'd tried to get a doll dress over her head—sitting on the back of the gray couch, waiting to bat Easy's tail whenever she walked by. I remember her shape, that sinewy silhouette, as it caught itself darkly before the sliding glass door to the green light of the garden at the back of our first Brooklyn apartment on Willow Street. Like a proper sibling, I blamed her for things. When, at age four, I'd taken my unfulfilled desire for bangs into my own hands and hidden the chunk of hair I'd clipped from the not-so-center of my head under my bedroom chair, I declared the hair "Easy's hair" after it was discovered by my mom while she was vacuuming. I declared this, of course, as she stared like a cat, un-blinking, at the mini-Mohawk sticking up like a unicorn horn from my head.

I was four and a half when Easy suddenly collapsed in the kitchen. For years, I heard the sound of her nails trying to catch the floor—her last great act of life. My mother took her to the animal hospital in midtown Manhattan, and I never saw her again. *Cancer* is a word they used. But how can a word so invisibly wickedly fill a dog up?

Did Easy remember my mother's miscarriage? I don't. I don't remember a lot of things that must remember me. My clenched, chubby baby fists and sopping, teething mouth inevitably filled with Easy's hair. I don't remember walks with her or touching her, hugging her, feeling her against me, the resident human baby. I don't remember her smell. I don't remember having a particular bond, more that we shared the same dashing parents and tidy, tasteful living room. This is pretty well illustrated in the numerous, now dilapidated, red photo albums still kept in my parents' bookcase on the lowest shelf under all the architecture books. There are some photos of Easy and, once I came along, a million of me, but only a couple, I recall, of us together. Easy possessed the same enigmatic, well-groomed nature as my parents and left me in my clunky do-it-yourself-bang mess. I don't remember her making me feel better about anything—or worse. She was an animal, and I remember her as such—snout, nails, hair. But what I remember best is what it felt like to be without her when she was gone.

A dog is nothing then. A dog is a dream I once had. A disappearance. A dog-shaped hole in an empty house.

On April 1, 1980, one week after Easy died, my family moved from our rental apartment on Willow Street around the corner to our purchased brownstone apartment on Pierrepont Street, where we lived in the top two floors. We shifted from life in the low, dark garden up into the big bright rectangle of sky. My parents bought the building with their friends the Vases: Meg, a concert pianist; George (who also played the piano), a Hungarian neurologist; and their musically gifted kids, Steven (cello) and Becky (piano), four and six years older than I was. It was unusual for the sound of their concert grand not to be skittering up through the floorboards, taking hold of teacups, ankle bones, and houseplants with the tiniest vibrations. Over the years, my parents and I developed the game of guessing which Vas was playing based on the music we heard. My mom always seemed to know best.

The building was sectioned into four separate units, one on

each floor, so we essentially moved into a construction zone, living in the house while whole walls were struck down and before all the rooms as we'd know them were made. We walked on thick, dirty paper and greeted each other through plastic walls like Elliott's family in *E. T.* We slept as a threesome all over the place, camping out wherever was cleanest and safest. My parents still talk about how awful that period was, living amid the mess, but, as the kid, I remember it as exciting, and probably only a quarter as long as it actually was. What I don't remember is the sadness that they must have felt after losing Easy, their first baby, and the pregnancy, what would have been their third baby. Though maybe that all quietly fits under the "awful" umbrella of which my parents speak. For reasons I believe were seeded long before they were born, the tendency in my family and my family's families has been to swallow hard around hard things, to will big emotions back down. From my earliest memories, I gauged how good or bad things were by how quiet it got, how absent the bodies were around me, how fast they moved, as if motion could literally propel the bad stuff away. When things were good, bodies calmed so that I could see them. We could all go back to trying to look each other in the eyes.

Maybe it was easier that we'd moved so quickly away from that house where the dog-shaped hole still lay—the baby-shaped hole, too. Everyone got busy building a new home, a space that never knew the dog or the womb or the pain that losing both must have left. Our new life on Pierrepont Street moved forward as if there'd never been a dog or the hope for any other children but me. Easy never set foot in our Pierrepont Street home, and so there was nothing to divine from her absence there. No haunting traces. Only paint chips and sawdust to pick up. And what about their third? He or she, too, had scurried off with Easy now into the driving quiet. What *didn't* I miss about the miscarriage I'd missed? *Where in a body does grief you dare not speak of go?* Was it grief that grew a mass on my cousin Morley's spine, years after her sister Anne died sleepwalking out of a fourth-story window? Was it grief that turned the ladybug on the dead body of a dear friend's mother into her mother? Grief holds the body itself hostage sometimes. Why not a house, too?

I am sure my parents worked hard to keep their sadness over having lost a pregnancy and a dear dog from me. I was, after all, only four. But as a mom, I know my own version of that instinct now around delivering emotionally heavy news—the difficulty in deciding what kids need to know and what they don't. But as a former four-year-old, I also know how much tiny bones can carry even when they don't fully grasp what's going on. I know how much one small witness can see, if not explain. I know what it is to be the only child detective in the house, the only one searching for something with a name.

I looked for Easy so hard in that new house, it was as if she were more real to me than ever. Even in her absence, she, the Dog, my warm and puzzling disappeared Dog-Sister, was the link I knew to sensation, that terrifying knee-dip of a thing you feel could kill you if you feel it (but give it a chance and there's grace). And it *was* too much to feel anything back then. It would be for decades. But the Dog was gone. And the Dog had become the place for the too-much feeling to go. What now? Without her, what disorderly creature might come out of me?

Where are you, Dog? Is it possible when our mom put you in the car that you never came out? I've been on those Voyages to Nowhere, Dog. Is that what happened? Instead of Nowhere, you accidentally went Somewhere? Why don't you come when I call? We have to walk up three flights of stairs now. Can you do stairs? Can you hear me? Can't you hear me calling your name?

Agatha 1: Dog of Death

(1980–1980)

I t took around a year for my new bedroom at Pierrepont to be in good enough shape for me to stop camping out with my parents and move in. The rest of the house came after. As my dad told me, "We really wanted to get your room done. We didn't want to stunt growth!" Once my street-side perch was mine, I lived in it like it *was* me. It was my favorite place on Earth. I played with my plastic horses and stuffed animals for hours on the white shag rug, making a boat out of my white wrought-iron twin bed with the brass finials that gently jingled when you turned over, sometimes knocking the animals off into the white shag ocean just for the opportunity to save them. The room had two windows with wooden shutters and striped pink floral cushioned window seats, one twice as long as the other. I didn't know it then, but the longer one would be the seat on which I would spend much of my first eighteen years, suspiciously spying into the lit-up wall of apartments smack-dab across the street like a budding Jimmy Stewart in *Rear Window*, or peering left to try to catch a tugboat working a big barge nimbly upriver, or waiting—waiting for my dad to come home from work, for someone I knew to walk by, for my boyfriend to come pick me up for a date. But for now there was a closet of clothes that would see me all the way from Beatrix Potter to Axl Rose. My domestic-goddess mom sewed and smocked many early dresses for me while she sat with other moms on the benches of the Pierrepont Playground, watching me climb the old jungle gym, hanging upside down until my underwear showed. One of her more memorable creations was matching panda outfits she sewed out of sweatshirt material for my best friend, Harriet, and me. If it still fit, I'd wear it.

It was inside this phosphorescent planet-maker of a room where I also first met my imaginary friends, Brownie and Little Miss Tiny. They lived inside the smaller window seat on the left. Brownie, an angelic brown furball with no face, and Little Miss Tiny, a terribly naughty knockoff of Kay Thompson's Eloise, only very, *very* tiny. When she did bad things, like eat my mother's baking chocolate, I would throw her out my window as punishment because she would only break both her legs, not *die*. For my psychoanalytic readers, the only other biographical details I can tell you about them are that they shared the same father and he lived in Florida. It's unclear to me if I thought of myself as their mother, but I don't think so. I think they were motherless. I don't remember when they first appeared—as with being born into a house with a dog in it, it seemed like they'd always been there, the invisible warp threads of the tapestry against which I was made—but I gather it was around the same time I moved into my room and there was a safe place for me to keep them. It had been more than a year since Easy had died, and while I don't remember when I told my parents about them, I gather the news had something to do with our next dog, my first puppy, Agatha.

Agatha was a black Scottish terrier. My parents gave her to me for Christmas. I wanted to name her Puddles because she immediately peed on the floor and that's how a six-year-old mind works, but my parents had their hearts set on Agatha, a suggestion made by friends over dinner one night. (Agatha Christie was known to have Scottish terriers, though perhaps the most famous Scottie that ever lived was Fala, President Franklin Roosevelt's dutiful companion during World War II.) Anyway, it would have been a pretty steep plunge from Ysé to Puddles.

Agatha was tiny and black and would be mine for the rest of my life. She'd follow me around the house and to school and wait for me by the door until I came out and walk back home with me. She'd get to know my teachers and my friends and the pigeons scattered on the scaffolding, and everyone would know her because we would be the Dog and the Girl. Our love would be famous. She would be on the cover of magazines, and when it came time, she would choose my husband for me, hold out her thick little paw and cry, "*Him!*"

In one of the only pictures I have of her, she's curled into a comma on the pillow next to my head. My plaid flannel pajamas alone tell me it's winter. I have freckles, no front teeth, and a very tall forehead, always somehow accentuated by my characteristic middle part. The fact that my cheeks are flushed and I'm in my parents' bed tells me I'm sick, because that's where I always spent sick days. Our only TV was in their room (until I was fourteen and had my first boyfriend and we wanted to watch movies together and my parents decided we would not be doing that while lying together in their bed and so moved it down to the living room in a neatly disguised cabinet under the books). From those same pillows, over the next decade, my mom, my dad, and I would watch every episode of *Miami Vice*, *The Cosby Show*, *The Wonder Years*, and *Seinfeld* together, though at some point I grew big enough that one of us had to move to a chair. I watched every episode of *Little House on the Prairie*, *Punky Brewster*, and *Beverly Hills, 90210* (which my mom called "teen slime") by myself. Although it's possible that in this picture I was just tired from Puppy Christmas, the best Christmas there ever was. It's possible my thoughts went straight to sickness here because what we didn't yet know when the picture was taken, but would learn as soon as the first night we had her, was that Agatha was sick. My father picked her up from a pet store on Long Island, back when we didn't know better. Her entire litter had parvovirus. Just a few days after he brought her home, she'd stopped eating and drinking and had to be euthanized.

I'd never had a puppy before, just an old dog that fell and died, but, as far as I could tell, puppies were the best time of the day. In those few days, we leaned into each other as hard as sea otters holding each other's feet so as not to drift away from each other while sleeping. Then my mom took her to the animal hospital and I never saw her again. I must have known this, and my parents must have understood how sick she was, but I don't remember knowing this myself. I don't remember her leaving or being taken. I don't remember a last kiss or a last touch. I don't remember going to the window to watch my puppy disappear. Isn't that how you keep the sad things away? What you don't see isn't real.

When the vet called to give my mom the news, I couldn't see her standing at the kitchen phone around the corner, but I could hear how her voice warped as she tried to take in the news and stop the tears. She hung up and walked into the living room, where I sat, already knowing and not knowing—not *wanting* to know. The first thing I did when I saw her face was laugh. I'd never seen her cry before, not that I remembered, anyway, and my whole body tapped out at the sight of her crooked-head-dead-dog crying face and the evidence before me that a mom could be hurt or sad or anything other than a mom at all. Up until then, she'd been my most dutiful mystery. I didn't always know what I knew about her, or what I didn't, or what there was to know, but I knew how to make her happy, so that's what I, the good dog, sank my teeth into in those early years of treading water, of not fully understanding in the midst of a wave which direction was up. Who were these people life had positioned around me? Why them? Why me? I tried to keep my mother's vibrant, funny, blinking beauty, the beauty everywhere, in its place. I tried not to disturb it. So when I saw her gnarled face coming toward me that slow rake of a day, I laughed at the discomfort of spotting devastation where devastation wasn't meant to exist. Then I cried, because my puppy was dead and how can dead happen to a puppy? How can a Christmas present *die*?

You can't go yet, puppy, not when our room is just ready, but you aren't lying. I've looked everywhere. There's only dog hair where the dog once was. Why didn't you tell me while you were so quickly here? A dog is death. A dog is abandonment. A dog is a mother with a crooked-head-dead-dog face for a face.

Agatha 2: Dog of Love

(1980-1993)

My parents must have heard the theory that the best way to mourn a dog is to replace it as soon as possible with the exact same breed, because even before the period of parvovirus contamination in our house had passed, we picked out another Scottie puppy, brindle this time, and from a responsible breeder in White Plains whose pups, we were promised, were exceptionally healthy. The three of us drove together to pick her out from the litter of puppies who'd been given apple names. We were led down to a basement of plush plum wall-to-wall carpet dotted with little black full-bellied bundles rolling around on top of each other like piglets. I don't know what I loved more in that moment—the puppies or the wall-to-wall carpet. But pretty soon I was up to my ears in both, luxuriating in the thick shag, letting puppies tumble all over me. There was a door with a tall mirror in which the carpet appeared infinite and I watched myself, the Puppy Queen, conducting my tiny charges.

I wanted the one who walked over, curled up in my lap, and fell asleep. My dad wanted the one who peed on him. "*That's* character," he said. So we went with character. She was the runt of the litter, little Ida Red. Agatha 1 hadn't lived long enough to fully embody her name, I guess, so we named her Agatha 2. Though we picked her out that day, we had to leave her there for another thirty days to ensure our house was virus free. I don't remember that period of waiting at home because I don't think I ever left that heavenly, cushy, puppy-stinking basement. It's the room that padded my dreams and held me until the dog could.

There had been Easy and, ever so briefly, Agatha 1, of course, but neither had been the dog that lodged in my heart, the dog that buried its bones between my bones. Agatha 2 was that dog. Perhaps because I was an only child, our bond took on such ravishing weight, but when I first smelled the heat of her breath on my face, I knew I'd been born to know her and she'd been born to know me. She slept in my boat bed (though her legs were too short to reach—I had to lift her), watched me rescue all of the stuffed animals who fell from it, followed me past the vegetable garden onto the granite creek wall during those big, sandy Long Island Sound summers my family spent living by the ocean while Agatha and I looked for fiddler crabs if the tide was low and eels if it was high. She spied on the grown-ups with me, sat with her hot August coat against my knee as I pulled up grass to bite the white roots while trying to come up with reasons why grown-up faces didn't always seem to match the hearts I could hear underneath. Was anyone else trying to see past happy to something more humming, something more real? What *was* real, anyway? Was Agatha? There were days I embodied her so fully that adults seemed to look at me with a pity that suggested I might well have dreamed her up.

Phantom or not, she was as good company to me as any

human—she was the *best*. I used to find her on her kilim pillow under the piano during my parents' dinner parties. While the adult world swirled like a carousel around us, lights smeared into streamers of fabric, lips, food, and drinks, we'd start up our own conversations, pick up wherever we'd left off. We settled many matters under the black canopy of that trusty, not-so-tuned baby grand. Even though I took lessons for a few years, it always functioned more as a dog-girl fort than an instrument. While most of the time we followed along together in the upright world of humans, under that piano was the site of my boldest entries into the world of Dog—Our World, I called it. A world of two. I know she understood every word I ever told her—not because she was a particularly scholarly Scottie, choosing to communicate almost chiefly through body language and unspoken, knowing looks, but because I *needed* her to understand.

The world I grew up in was a beautiful world. Brooklyn Heights is a historic waterfront neighborhood, one that people, whether they're from the borough's other districts or not, loved to tell me wasn't "*real* Brooklyn." It's full of stately old brownstones with their well-appointed façades and window boxes dripping through spring. A handful of its quiet, tree-lined residential streets lead grandly west to the Promenade, a roughly half-mile-long, cantilevered walkway over the Brooklyn-Queens Expressway that holds you up and out before the billowed bend of downtown Manhattan like you might just be standing before God. The neighborhood is bespeckled with magical private gardens that popped up regularly in print (my dad's own enchanting roof deck included)—the people who owned them, too. Brooklyn Heights was an enchanting place to grow up, but, as far as I could see, it was also a world that tended toward stiff lips and alcohol over transparency and self-reflection. A world—a time, too, perhaps—that championed achievement, and less so emotional truth. Nothing was named in this beautiful world. We were what we put on every day. We were the stories we told. We were the food, the wine, the linens.

There's a strength to this approach, a relentlessness of survival and success, and I learned early that this works for some, that this, for some, will always be enough—for others, would be more than enough, and more than they had. I also learned that this was not what I needed, that there is a danger, even, when the choreography of life depends upon the denial of so much of the rest, of all that is messy and *un*deniable—of all that is human. *Success* even becomes a wicked word when your own definition of it is different from that of the ones hoping for you to succeed, when it becomes clear that it's *you* who is different.

You can't teach what wasn't taught to you, and from what I know of their childhoods, my parents both grew up in kind, devoted families that worked hard, but emotional depth wasn't at the root of them. Feelings were less the priority than generosity and good character. To feel was to need and to need was messy. But I felt things profoundly from the beginning. If I was happy or sad, I felt it in my cells' cells—cells I possessed without a clue from where they came. Despite being surrounded by my own devoted family, it was Agatha who I felt understood me in the way only blood does. It was she with whom I tried to make sense of our insular, privileged world. This was all the evidence I needed to prove this mom and dad who lived at Pierrepont Street with me were not my real ones. When I was six or seven, Agatha and I finally got up the nerve to say to them, our stomachs full of twigs, "It's okay to tell us now."

"Tell you *what*?" they asked.

"That we're adopted."

I think they must have delighted in this weird little question from their weird little girl who spent less time with humans than her dog, but I meant it. I had just *so* much feeling and no idea as to where it all came from, where it could all go.

Be the dog, I could suddenly feel my bones go. Dogs are a gateway, an uplift. A clear and present language. *Yes. No. Good. Bad.* They beg for treats, not achievement. They meet your needy eyes with the reflection of your needy eyes rather than needy eyes of their own. A fixed pattern of delighted stars in the otherwise thumping dark, they hold stories on their insides, too. Why couldn't the dog hold mine?

It's a strange thing to feel so lucky to have grown up where I did, and with whom, and be all the madder for it, too. Perhaps to some degree we all feel that way about our beginnings—that necessary, intergalactic push-and-pull. We separate in order to grow. But separating for an only child is a particularly hefty leap. At least, it was for me. I wasn't ready to separate—not by a long shot. In human terms, I was too big a piece of my family's three-piece puzzle to be otherwise. I best knew Me in relation to Them, not as Me alone. I best knew Me as holding up my part of Us. For so long, I had felt like an elder myself. The only separating I'd done was split in two, not grow: I was Me unless Me felt too hard, then I was the dog. Agatha could hold and tolerate all the parts of me unsuitable for my human life, even when I returned to my human self; when days and all of their requisite relationships and outings beckoned me back in, she walked around with at least half of me still thrashing inside her.

My home of three was a quiet one, the loudest sound in it

often a piano concerto rising up through the floorboards and heating vents from the Vases'. When home, my dad was often in his study, though Agatha and I were always welcome to visit him. He'd take a break and teach us how to draw the plans for a house. We especially loved his miniature renderings of toilets and sinks and doors. My mother was often cooking, though Agatha and I were also always welcome to visit her. Sometimes we'd sit on the long steps to the deck and talk; sometimes she'd teach us how to chop garlic (never press it—that makes it too bitter; rather, dice it with a firm, seesawing blade) or cut vegetables on an angle for extra elegance. You should see her carve a cucumber into a turtle. Unless we had visitors to unite for or unless we were traveling, there was a lot of time the three of us were squirreled away in our separate quarters of the house, doing three different things under a single roof. Ours wasn't a family that gathered around board games, chatting through life's off-hours just to gobble up more time together. We mostly talked as life required it—at meals, at parties, at the requisite family transitions of dusk and dawn.

It seems to me that we only children end up with not only our birth parents but infinite ones—ourselves included. Without siblings to pinch-hit, if we're lucky, everyone does. If my cousin Libby thought I was being too cautious, she'd steal me away to her farm in Manton, Michigan, where we rode her horses bareback, always on the lookout for stray holes they might hook a hoof in, or take me canoeing on the Au Sable River to look for eagles. If Harriet's mom, Tina, thought my lunch was too healthy, she'd make me a big, fat Fluffernutter sandwich, marshmallow oozing onto the plate like a liquid ghost. Just when I thought I'd never know what it was like to have an older brother, my uncle

Stewart, who was seventeen when I was born, showed up with a light-up globe and an invitation to go ice skating. When I looked around and nobody human was there, I found me.

Of course, none of this made me an adult. In the most essential ways, I was still very much a little girl, and, as nature would have it, I was a good little girl to boot. I learned to say the right things even when they felt wrong. I learned to be fine. I learned to be deeply private. Held, not always heard. Celebrated, not always seen. Loved, not always known. And before I learned to write, I learned to be the dog. I learned to tell Agatha what I wondered and worried about most.

Are there wolves in New York City, Dog? If we leave our front door open, will they trot in their wounded snow? Can they climb stairs? Is it weird that I have imaginary friends? Is my vagina supposed to look like this? Does the middle finger mean something different in ballet? What are the names of everything? When you grow up are you going to drink crazy juice, too? Are there words for the faces my parents make when no one but I am watching? Why can't I ever stop laughing? Why does it feel so awful to turn so red? What if Dad is late? Does that mean he's dead? Can't I be you, Dog, full bellied, wet nosed, dreaming of kilim pillows covered in batter meant for cakes? Just for today, can't I be the prickliest part of your face?

Maybe a dog is a second chance. A dog is death and life. A dog is plush red carpet and fresh warm pee.

Brooklyn was a far cry from the Scottish Highlands, where Agatha's ancestors were bred to hunt rats, foxes, and badgers, but she seemed to do American pavement and squirrels just fine. Our cat, Pearl, learned to navigate Agatha's instinct to chase more shrewdly than I've seen any cat do since or before. I once saw her pull off a move only previously performed on *Tom & Jerry*. As Agatha barreled down the living room floor, Pearl waited for the perfect moment to catapult herself into the air, floating for the exact amount of time it took for Agatha to obliviously run under her, and while Pearl casually tiptoed upstairs, Agatha frantically sniff-searched for her for what seemed like the rest of the day.

Agatha's eyebrows, if they are even called eyebrows on a dog, were like the epaulets on a French Republican Guardsman. They shifted and bounced and quivered as she responded to the world, her brown eyes peering out from under them like big polished raisins. Probably because I'd always wanted one, but also because of her funny size—short legs, barrel body, large head—she reminded me of a little horse, and so, sometimes, I treated her like one. I taught her to jump over my extended leg like my very own urban show pony. There was nothing my dad loved more, which I knew because he would nostril-laugh, and there was nothing I loved more than his nostril laugh. Together, we wrote my first poem:

DOG LIPS by Chloe and her dad, 1983
Dog lips, dog lips,
Black and slimy,
Gosh O Golly,
Aren't they grimy?

Agatha was the last purebred dog I ever had, and for a purebred, she was a little rough around the edges. She was the runt, after all. According to its breed standard, the Scottie is a "small, compact, short-legged, sturdily-built dog of good bone and substance. The Scottie's head is long in proportion to his size. He has a hard, wiry, weather-resistant coat and a thick-set, cobby body which is hung between short, heavy legs. These characteristics, joined with his very special keen, piercing, 'varminty' expression, and his erect ears and tail are salient features of the breed. The Scottish Terrier's bold, confident, dignified aspect exemplifies power in a small package." Agatha's traits followed this definition loosely—in other words, anyone would have recognized her, on sight, as a Scottie. But her quirks brazenly cemented the fact that no one from Westminster ever came knocking on our door. If a Scottie's head is "long in proportion to his size," Agatha's was double long. She seemed to be *all* head. Her tail was like a misfit carrot, a slight crook near the base. Terriers are known for their spirited nature, enormous personalities stuffed into taut little bodies, and Agatha was spirited, but not with the aggression that can come attached. The American Kennel Club describes the Scottie temperament as "a determined and thoughtful dog whose 'heads up, tails up' attitude in the ring should convey both fire and control. The Scottish Terrier, while loving and gentle with people, can be aggressive with other dogs. He should exude ruggedness and power, living up to his nickname, the 'Diehard.'" There was nothing fiery or controlled about Agatha. She was generally a good pup who loved her humans so much she seemed a little human herself. Her nickname might as well have been the "Lovehard."

Agatha could sit, lie down, give me her paw, and generally make the world better. She had a few run-ins with things she shouldn't have eaten, including a pack of Clorets gum from my grandmother's purse and an entire package of pancake mix that was wrapped under our Christmas tree one year. She crawled under our dining room table and stayed there for a few days; the sounds coming from her belly were monsters. But she was generally a little pleaser of a dog. I could make her ears go submissively flat just by looking at her, just by saying her name, whatever a name is to a dog but a particularly triggering scoop of human breath.

I've heard it said that most dogs don't know their names, they just know tones of voice, routines, and food sources. Though we're told when training them always to use their names, not nicknames, and quick one-word commands, not sentences, we so often talk to them like they're people or shove commands into the middle of conversations that experts say they end up thinking their name isn't Scout, but ScoutGetYourPaws-OfftheCounterWhatDoYouThinkofTheseShoes? I've come to think of these as their dog names, as opposed to the ones we give them, their human names. If this is true, Agatha's dog name was undoubtedly AgathaCan'tIBeYouforToday? For a while I thought it was hilarious to call her with names that merely rhymed with Agatha to test her intelligence (or so I thought). "Bagatha!" I'd yell, or "Zagatha!" She, of course, came to them all. My grandfather Seaweed (so named by his fishing buddies after a particularly seaweed-filled haul), who rarely called anyone by their actual name, called Agatha "Althea." But he also called me Chloe-Clump. No matter. I came when he called, too. So maybe we're not that different around this, humans and dogs. Maybe we just need the impression of love on the other end— tones of voice, routines, and food sources, too. After all, these are the names I've responded to in my four decades as Chloe:

Chloe, Chloe-Clump, Chlo, Cho-lee, Chuh-lo-ee, Chi-lo-hey, Chloesha, Muffin, Miss Bland, Mrs. Shaw, Chica, Sweets, Babe, Mom, Mommy, Mama, MomDoYouHaveAnySnacks? And perhaps it was my relationship with Agatha, but all that has ever mattered is with what quantity of love they came.

Like many friends' houses I frequented in my 1970s–1990s Brooklyn youth, our house on Pierrepont Street was the kind of house you wouldn't necessarily have known a child or a dog lived in unless you opened my bedroom door. (By contrast, you might wonder as you walk into my house today if anyone *but* children and dogs live here.) I regularly used the word *vestibule* by age five because we had one. The first thing you saw upon entering our vestibule was a Tiffany grandfather clock, thought to be more than a hundred years old, purchased at auction in Los Angeles by my paternal great-great-grandfather. When it was wound, toward the top, a moon with a face told you which lunar phase you were in.

A first set of stairs took you up to the main floor, which was essentially one long room, the living room and dining room split in two by the baby grand piano and small sitting area. At the back of the apartment, around the corner on the left side of the dining room, was our kitchen, the tiniest room in the house—a detail made more intriguing by the fact that my mom is the best self-trained cook I know.

As you rounded the bottom step of the staircase leading to the second floor, there on your left beneath the big skylight hung one of the only pieces of potential first-floor evidence that this was the house of a child: my portrait. In it, I'm wearing a pink dress with embroidered flowers, and at the bottom of the painting, in light brown scrawl, it says, *A Joy*. Though the letters strike me as somewhat mystical now in light of my genetic predisposition to appear cheerful, to be fine, they weren't descriptive. The artist's name was Alison Joy. As I sat for her, Alison had quickly discovered the best way to get me to keep still was to place her teeny Yorkshire terrier in my lap.

Our bedrooms—mine over Pierrepont Street, my parents' over the deck—and our bathrooms and my mom's study, with its desk, bookshelf, and twin guest bed, took up the top floor of the house. Because of the skylight up there, I always knew when it was raining before I even got out of bed. I've always loved those percussive sounds of weather and science.

Though it was a house with grapefruit spoons and artwork from the galleries of London, it wasn't fancy in the way some houses can feel untouchable and uncomfortable. It was personally elegant. My dad hammered horizontal rows of half-inch half rounds (one every foot or so) to the stair walls and painted the entire surface with an ochre sponge technique to recall something warm and ancient, like a wall you might come upon down a towering Italian alley. He painted with a similar technique, though in a frothy, dusty green, on the wall behind their bed.

Each of their paintings or pieces of furniture came from a trip or a friend or a family member or had to be shipped in a dramatic enough fashion so as to necessitate a colorful, corresponding tale to be told with props and pictures over one of my mom's knockout meals served on knockout plates over a knockout table setting in front of my dad's staggering garden.

My parents' undeniable savvy for staging, engaging all of the senses in passing through or settling into a room, is thanks solely to what I have come to think of as their shared superpower: they look at a space and—poof!—outrageous beauty.

The apartment's back wall was essentially a row of tall French doors that opened up to the magnificent urban garden my dad quietly grew over the years. It started with two big planters and a trellis between them, overhead. Two benches faced each other beneath. After that, any time you turned your back, pot after pot after pot popped up like a gathering botanical army.

For a period during my middle school years, we had two blue cots for deck camping. I had more than a few sleepovers out there, during which I tried so hard to fit Agatha into my sleeping bag. She never liked sleeping under the covers though. She was happiest sleeping on my feet. We stopped inviting her on those sleepless urban sleep-outs when the morning squirrel activity proved too electrifying. By a certain point in her life, you could say to her "Mr. Squirrel" in any room of the house and she'd run to the nearest window and lift her paw, the terrier in her ever on point.

Meals in my house were never just occasions to refuel the body and press on; they were opportunities for more beauty. Early in my parents' marriage, my mother would choose one thing and prepare it over and over until perfect, her Hollandaise stretch perhaps most memorable for the weight they both put on. Her mac 'n' cheese was never from a box or orange. It was white and had several kinds of cheeses, a from-scratch bécha-mel, and bread crumbs, also homemade. Nothing she made ever came out of a box—in fact, her meals were often created from ingredients procured not only from several different stores but several different boroughs. And that was just a regular old Tuesday dinner for three. You should have seen their parties.

Like their house, their parties were never ostentatious or over-the-top affairs but dazzling domestic ballets, every one a perfectly choreographed performance that often required days of prep. I knew it was really something special if my dad got the floor waxer out, the wonderful, rich smell of which was the industrial olfactory counterpart to my mom's gourmet goings-on just around the corner in the kitchen. The floor would be so slippery right after that that Agatha and I would wipe out in front of the World's Tallest Mirror, otherwise known as the Victorian-era pier mirror from my great-grandmother's house in Saginaw, Michigan, which hung on the wall of our dining room and went all the way to the ceiling like one of the Twin Towers framed in gold.

I often took the role of Coat-Check Girl, greeting the guests at the front door to take coats before transforming into Hors d'Oeuvres Passer on the way back upstairs. I liked having these little jobs. They gave me something to do, someone to be other than Daughter. They gave me something to focus on when out and about on the social front lines, where I was not naturally inclined to go. Where I *was* naturally inclined to go was up to my room or to the pillow under the piano with Agatha. Even when I wasn't physically under the piano with her, when I was talking to one of my parents' friends (I always had my favorites), it felt like that was where I was looking out from, watching myself navigate the rogue waves of the adult world from inside the hale-hearted, hairy armor of the dog. We were, of course, the two biggest threats to the beautiful world we were in. Nothing says *mess* like a dog and her kid. Though *the cat* is the one who scratched my parents' record collection *and* the yellow couch covered in Knoll wool weave *and* peed on the dining room banquette, the only time in my life I've ever heard my mom swear was when Agatha had diarrhea all over the white living room rug. It was right before we left for school. She threw her keys down as hard as she could and yelled, "*Shit!*" She wasn't wrong. Agatha and I were threats, all right, but we were also the most adaptive. Me, from the womb; she, from the wolf. We were a well-trained pair. Both of us treat-oriented, we knew how to make our humans happy. She was rewarded with biscuits; me, with approval.

During their parties was my favorite time to be falling asleep in my bed, typically a fraught transition for me into darkness. All the rosy voices, the dinging of china and glass, were like a lifeline connecting my dark World of One to the greater light of life, humankind. I felt held by the space around me, not swallowed by it. I could be a little less vigilant about my preventative evening routine of biting a few threads from my beloved blanket, my Night-Night; soaking them with saliva; and forming them into little balls I called "fuzzies" that I would stick to my face. As I lost myself to the tickly sensation of their drying against my skin, solidifying into a kind of protective shield, and sucked my right index and middle fingers, I'd place my great, big stuffed sheepdog, Montgomery, on top of my head. I would have done so with Agatha would she have let me. But she preferred to keep watch from the foot of the bed. And like that, she and I would fuse into one—she the less-than Scottie, me the less-than girl. It was our shared superpower, after all: going dog.

The two other Brooklyn Heights homes I spent the most time in were Harriet's and Whitten's. They lived next door to each other on Garden Place, a one-block street where it seemed every kid in the neighborhood lived. Halloween was an epic affair. If Harriet was a sister in my sibling-less life, then Whitten was undoubtedly a brother. They were both there before memories were, even: my bustling pack of little humans.

Whitten's mom, Eileen, and my mom started a catering business together in 1980 called Good Taste. They cooked out of Eileen's kitchen, which was bigger than ours, so Whitten and I spent countless afternoons at his house, watching *He-Man* in the attic, building pillow forts, calling each other *dork* and *spaz*, and spying on our mothers as they whisked and simmered and chopped three floors down. Whitten had red hair and freckles, and he and I went back and forth *like*-liking each other for years, eventually dating and marrying others without somehow ever sharing a single kiss. He was funny and a little reckless. He made me feel tough like a brother might, giving me dead arms and noogies, always stopping a beat or two past my "Mercy!"

When we were nine or ten, Whitten wrote down a phone number on a piece of paper, told me it was a sex hotline and that he'd called it. Twice. I put the paper in my pocket before I could feel the feeling of being in a body and we snuck down to the first floor, sliding on our bellies through the dining room to get as close as possible to our mothers without their knowing, the ultimate goal being under the table they were working on. If we made it, it was Mission Accomplished!

"Ha! Ha!" we'd say, jumping up.

"Oh *my!*" they always said. "We had *no* idea, you little sneaks!"

We'd run back upstairs, Shadow, Whitten's black Lab, following only partway up. It was a lot of stairs for a good, big dog, which brings me to the downside of our moms' working such long hours at his house: no Agatha. Shadow was one of a handful of auxiliary dogs I made do with—and he was great. So were Harriet's dog, Carmella the bloodhound, and my friend Katherine's dog, Tessie the border collie. But they weren't Agatha. No dog was. How could they be when she functioned as the very pericardium of my heart? A dog is our bridge to inside ourselves, a song of fixed, singular yearning.

One day, when we were nine or ten, we sat on the big brown pillows in the attic and made ourselves bored. Whitten took the toy wooden gun his grandfather had made off the shelf and aimed it at me, up close. The nail at the tip of the gun which you were meant to aim with by centering it in the loop of the screw eye up near your face, went up my nose a little and scraped the underside of my nostril. I stuck a finger to the scrape and there was blood. I got a tissue. The blood stopped. More bored.

"Let's count to three and both pull down our pants," Whitten said.

A dog would never say that.

"Nope," I said.

"*C'mon.* It'll be fair because we'll both be doing it."

"Nope."

"What about sitting down in front of each other with our legs out and just pulling our shorts to the side super quick?"

He sat down and demonstrated without actually moving the fabric.

"*Fine,*" I said.

"Okay," he said. "Sit like me."

We got into position.

"I'm going to count to three," he said.

My stomach was a chipmunk.

"One, two, three."

Nothing. No one moved. No one did a thing. We went through this routine several times: the counting, the stomachs, the nothing. After the third or fourth round, Whitten ran to the intercom, pulled down the switch, and sent his voice booming into every room of the four-story house, "Chloe showed me her vagina!"

It took a second before we heard the sound of two mothers running for their lives, but here they came! I told them I didn't show him *anything*. He told them I did. We were asked to play downstairs for the rest of the afternoon.

When my mom and I got home, I remembered the number in my pocket. I went upstairs and unfolded it. This was something new. It made me feel a little sick to look at those numbers, and a little magic, like I'd stolen a rock from the moon. I went into my parents' room, picked up the phone, and dialed. The woman's voice on the recording gave a few explicit options and told me how to proceed in a low, breathy voice. I sat on my mom's side of the bed, stock-still as a zoo bison mouthing its fence. I didn't understand everything she said or why she would say it, but I hung up and called my friend Katherine and gave her the number. Katherine called the number, then gave it to her little sister, Helen, who called it, too. Then Katherine and Helen's mom, Anne, called my mom to tell her that they'd gotten a sex hotline number from me. *Me*, still *way* too young to know what a body was, what *my* body was, what it would be capable of taking in one day, and pushing out.

What is a body, Dog? A boy told me he saw my earwax and I turned the color of the reddest step on the red stairs the high schoolers all hang out on. Do you blush, Dog? What did that sex hotline lady say again? I can't remember. I can keep people happy by needing nothing. If I could just make myself invisible, Dog. How?

My mom talked to me. She wasn't so mad, just steady and teaching and probably a little embarrassed. I called Anne and apologized. Anne laughed. Her laugh always had such love in it.

When I hung up, I told my mom again, "I didn't show Whitten *anything.*"

And I didn't. And you know it, Whitten Morris. You dog, you.

In my memory, Agatha 1 had lived longer than a few days—at least for a few weeks—and so I thought my earliest memories of puppyhood were somehow more about her, my *first* puppy, than about Agatha 2, my second. But, in fact, all of my memories outside that one Christmas picture of Agatha 1 are of Agatha 2. That must be why we dropped the 2 eventually. When my parents and I want to say something about Agatha 1, we say Agatha 1, but when we want to say something about Agatha 2, we simply say Agatha, like she was the canine Cher or Madonna of her time.

Whenever I made a new friend, or eventually, boyfriend, Agatha was the first special thing I wanted them to meet. My parents and my room were second and third. Whenever I spend time going through old letters and yearbooks, I am always amazed at all the references to Agatha. I know people liked her—she was very likable, except for maybe when she bit my cousin Caitlin once. (Sorry, Caitlin.) You know how it sometimes goes with tiny fingers and terriers. But more, they knew how much I loved her, and because they loved me, they knew to include her, they knew that to mention her was to honor and inhabit my world. From a letter my high school sweetheart wrote me once he'd moved on to college: "How is little Agatha? You have to pet her for me. You know I really am quite fond of her." Aside from sounding remarkably like a Jane Austen love interest here, he had a sweet relationship with her but didn't come from a dog or pet kind of family, and so he didn't just jump all in at the sight of a dog like I did. But he knew. If you were going to love me, or be loved by me, you'd better love, or at least pretend to love, Agatha.

On our family's annual summer car trips to Michigan, she would lie on the seat next to me, snug right up against my leg. I remember being particularly delighted that she was the exact length of the depth of the seat. We had obviously chosen the right puppy. The rainbow threads of the friendship bracelets I made for fifteen hours straight, pinning them to the back of the headrest, would sometimes land on her and tickle her epaulets until they woke her. "Sorry!" I'd whisper. "We're not there yet. You can go back to sleep." Michigan is where she learned to swim, though I wouldn't have called her a big swimmer in her day. She preferred for me to pull her around in a little yellow-and-blue blow-up boat that must have been made of Teflon to withstand those tough little terrier nails.

In addition to our annual pilgrimage to Michigan, from ages ten through twelve, I spent summers at Camp Treetops in Lake Placid, New York, the handsome geological hotbed of the Adirondacks. They were dogless summers on a working farm—no dogs that I remember but plenty of farm animals, a thrilling anomaly to this city-clad girl. Campers maintained the crops and animals over the summer, while students at the adjoining North Country School maintained the crops and animals over the winter. It also offered all the typical camp-y stuff you'd expect: swimming, canoeing, hiking, riding, square dancing, sleeping in tents under mosquito nets. We hiked in the dark to reach a summit for sunrise, sticking close, singing songs to scare the bears. We lived off the land, eating almost nothing but what we'd learned to find in nature from Millie, a magical camp mother of sorts. She cooked blueberry fritters that are still the best things I've ever eaten. We roamed freely, got as muddy as possible after the big rains, were allowed one shower a week (we swam in the lake daily) and no sugar, except for an ice-cream cone every Sunday and whatever contraband outsiders were able to sneak into our mail (once Harriet was able to get a stick of Juicy Fruit gum to me and I still don't know how; I can only assume the mail monitor was sick that day). For those almost eight weeks, I existed nowhere else but there. I had no history and no future. I carried no load but the muddied, wild bones of Camp Kid. In a childhood largely devoid of religion, this was my heaven on earth. I had no comfortable conceptions about what God was, but I believed in Camp Treetops wholeheartedly—cookie-sized blackfly welts sticky with vitamin E, the compost pile, all of it. The liberal way of life there reached a tenacious but untapped part of me. Despite my being a Brooklyn native, my bones always felt more like the bones of Laura Ingalls Wilder. I mean, did I really have what it took to weather a life in which my horse Bunny's galloping through a fence she didn't know was there meant that my dad had to end her with a rifle? I don't think so. But I could weed the carrots and bottle-feed the baby goats and pick clean the great hooves of a gray Appaloosa named Chief, the equine love of my life, all day long. Chief was as close as I could get to my Agatha away from home, which I needed those long camp summers. Though his massive barrel body could have contained about fifteen Agathas, their eyes both possessed the same beastly light as they shifted and dropped to better take me in. In that way you can't exactly explain why you love someone, from the moment I laid eyes on the gray Appaloosa with a black Mohawk, I saw potential for the camp version of my emotional center. To maximize our time together, I had to land him as a work job, one of the daily tasks we were assigned each week. There were cleaning up the boathouse, setting the tables for meals, weeding the garden, tending to the animals. We wrote our names down next to our top three preferences and were guaranteed one first choice per summer. As you can imagine, the horses were a hot commodity, as opposed to, say, the compost heap, the fumes of which regularly made campers make compost heaps of their own. But there was a clever, albeit revolting, way to go about this if you were dead set on a horse, like I was. If you logged one week at the compost pile or honey wagon (the camp-cute way of saying "horse shit"), you were promised your first choice the following week. Oh, the pounds of poop I hauled for Chief! The maggots I forked through the trenches! One deep gaze into his smoky, patella-sized eyeball and it was all worth it. I'd found my horse-dog, after all. He so vividly and strangely overfilled the camp-induced Agatha-shaped hole in my heart, I remember wondering if they'd disappear if they met, like they couldn't possibly exist simultaneously.

The truth was that every time I left for those two-month stints in the mountains, I feared what life would be like without my little fiery-nosed heart fluff of a compass. I was without the part of me that *was* me, the secrets scribbled inside the bright red cabin of my heart. Though what's clear to me now as I remember the loved, wild feel of those loving, wilding months is that my time at camp was the only period during her luminous, cobby-bodied reign when I simply needed her less. (But did she still need me?)

This, however, was not true of traveling, which presented the most paradoxical of family truths. The farther away I got from home, the more I longed for Agatha and our homespun notion of shelter, of normal. But traveling with my parents was also when we often had the most fun together. It was on trips when we felt less like a father, mother, and daughter playing out that tricky, tippy only-child routine and more like three friends making stories, memories, and jokes. We laughed like Canada geese together, whispered like three different-sized pinecones grown up on the same branch. One night at dinner in Paris, three chocolates came with the check. My mom said she didn't want hers, so my dad said I could have it, to which I said, "No, *you* have it," to which he said, "No, *you*." More than three decades later, we are still passing that chocolate (now in dust form and rubber-banded inside a small plastic bag) back and forth, taking turns depositing it in secret, to-be-discovered-later places in each other's homes.

Our travels were always organized around cultural sights and food, so vacations for me were on-the-move affairs. They weren't for resting or watching movies. They were for living and learning. My dad was like the human version of those headset tours you can now take, a steady, knowledgeable voice pointing out historical sites and infinitesimal architectural detail, including, sometimes, the particular angle at which we should plant our feet and tilt our heads to best view them, while my mom rifled through her purse for the newspaper clippings and renegade underground culinary books corresponding to the city we were currently in. There isn't a city we've visited that we didn't eat our way through—but like real foodies, bouncing between the classic oldies and off-the-beaten-path finds. While driving through the Texas Hill Country near my dad's childhood roots in Austin one Easter, we spent a good portion of a day following long, dusty roads across cattle guards and by fields and fields housing either longhorns or transcendent horizontal rainbows of flowers, in search of Rabke's in Willow City because my mom had read about the beef jerky there. It was so delicious we ordered it every Christmas for years.

Even so, it was between these blissful *Little House on the Prairie* summers when I started to become more aware of a growing discomfort between my bones, a convergence of feelings I couldn't pretend even Agatha would begin to understand. *Devastated*, *excited*, *terrified*, and *alarmed* are the words that come to mind, but if you'd asked me back then how I was feeling, I probably would have told you "nothing" or "weird." What I now recognize as the obsessive whip of anxiety, it's known to manifest itself quite differently at different ages. In toddlers, it can look like tantrums, emotions gone out of control, whereas in adolescents, it can creep up with extreme, excessive worry, hypervigilance, the need to control. According to these definitions, my anxiety didn't bubble up until after toddlerhood. I fit the adolescent definition to a T. Though I held myself together like a living statue, all you had to do was look at my horribly ravaged fingernails to consider what different story lurked beneath.

What was I feeling but trying not to feel? A spinning, smoky sphere around my stomach. The sensation shot up into my chest and out to the tips of my fingers and toes and out from between my legs, almost like the dreadful excitement that comes right before you hear bad news. But all the time. Other times, it felt like my stomach was outside my body trying to find a way back in. Persistently in my ear I could feel my heart thud and at the same time knew this was not something the dog could hear. I felt the loneliness of what e. e. cummings describes as "small as a world and as large as alone." A horse alone is a dead horse, they say. Is that this kind of alone? What was I thinking? I was worried about absolutely everything absolutely all of the time. If in times of creativity my imagination is a blessing, in times of anxiety it is my greatest curse. There is no dark scenario I have not played out from under the covers. Sharks can live outside water; wrestling dummies can come to murderous life—garden gnomes, too; without your knowing, strangers can live in your house for years, gradually befriending your dogs when you're out until even their calm demeanor can't be trusted; once the lights are out, knives can pretty much do what they want. I'm not a good candidate for a schooling in the rational or statistical. It doesn't help to tell me I'm safe when I'm not even safe in my head. I don't remember ever not being like this, and it's so global and persistent that I still have to regularly remind myself that not everyone experiences life this way. These are big, messy feelings for someone so outwardly controlled. I spent most of my time trying not to look the way I felt inside—human vs. dog. Dogs are as they are, while humans possess the dreadful gift of imagination, make-believe. A dog is a straight shooter, a practical, knowing beast. While I know that anxiety can manifest in a dog (thanks to us humans, no doubt), it's impossible for me to fathom what it's like for the dog inside of it. With what imagination do they shudder? The pictures I play out are vivid and thunderous. But how does this same act play out in a dog? Is fear without hypotheticals better or worse? If you can't explain the fear, where except everywhere can the fear go?

My body was an agonizing body to be in, to *want* to be in, to want to stay in. A dog is the predisposed portal away from any anguish there is.

But since the dog wasn't always with me anymore, as I grew and growth sometimes took me on bigger, longer journeys, I had to find alternatives to the dog, since one thing was certain: no longer was I able *not* to pay attention to these paralyzing feelings I was trying not to feel. They were feelings too big to fit inside the dog. And I was way too old now for imaginary friends. I hadn't seen them in years. So that's how I found myself carrying out particular behaviors in order to right the world, keep things in line. I don't know where these behaviors came from or why they became what they did, I just knew that they made my day feel better, they made me feel safer, more in control. I counted every time I swallowed. I clicked my teeth together every time our car passed a lamppost. I tied my hair to everything. *I am real; I am Me; I was here.* Depending on how good the cleaning staff was, there may still be quite a few strands of my hair knotted around doorknobs, railings, and a few sturdy bushes at Versailles. I walked like a horse. A sleek, black coat and long, powerful legs thundering under me. I flew planes from my passenger seat by never taking my eyes off the ground. I became Agatha when we were miles apart by never taking my eyes off the sky. I'd look at a star at night and imagine she saw it, too, the way I would years later with a boy. One day in Paris, we stumbled on a store called Agatha. Its logo was a Scottie. Everything else I'd learned about Parisian culture and cuisine stopped right there. It was the surest sign that Agatha was with me even then. Just as I carried her, the dog carried me. What I believed had been true all along.

The majority of summers after I was too old for camp (Treetops brilliantly cuts things off around puberty) but before I was old enough to get a job, were spent two hours outside of Brooklyn, in Stony Creek on the Connecticut shore, where Harriet's father's family had built a Victorian home more than a century ago. From the sloping lawn, you could see a handful of the Thimble Islands, an archipelago of granite bedrock islands named Kuttomquosh—or "the Beautiful Sea Rocks"—by the Mattabeseck Native Americans. Among the islands, the seventeenth-century pirate Captain Kidd is thought to have buried treasure. As school let out every summer, we'd pack up and move in just as the raccoon families who'd spent their spring on the porches moved out, baby by baby.

Harriet and her two sisters, Mimi and Amanda; and her parents, Tina and Ted Ells; and their three cats, Kissie, Coconut, and Kit Kat; and their dog, Carmella, filled that big Victorian right up. The Ellses also owned a tiny house across the street—a converted boathouse—that fit my family of three, plus Agatha and Pearl, perfectly. In and around this tiny house is the setting of easily half of my memories of Agatha, especially of her going up and down the metal spiral staircase ticky-tocky-ticky-tocky like a windup toy and grazing in the yard like a cow until she threw up.

The house had two floors that measured a total of around 250 square feet. Downstairs was a kitchen, a living space with a table and couch, and a bathroom; upstairs was one long room in which you could only stand upright at its very center, the highest point of the roof. On the floor was a double mattress for my parents and a single mattress for me. There was no air-conditioning, and, *oh*, it could get hot up there, but that's just how things were. *That* was *summer*. So was my mom's home-made peach ice cream and from-scratch pasta I'd steal off the broomstick from which it hung drying in the sun like rag-doll hair. We sweat through the night, waiting out the late bugs and beach parties, and woke early to run wild through the day. Tina's rule was that unless there was lightning, we had to stay outside. She finally installed a water fountain by the hose so we would stop asking to come in just for water, just for the sake of survival.

Aside from mandatory swimming lessons at the local middle school with a coach called Flipper, and roadside pop-ins to Mrs. Loxa's vegetable stand for fresh corn and tomatoes, and Sunday morning "doughnut cruises" on Ted's sailboat, its deck sticky from a dozen devoured crullers, we had no schedule to which we adhered. We rode our bikes to the penny candy store, speeding home in a jiffy if any boys looked our way, and back out to Big Brooklyn, the retired granite quarry, part of a family of quarries famous for a particular pink granite used to create, among other notable structures, the base of the Statue of Liberty. It had a real *Stand by Me* feel back there, like at any moment we might discover a dead body. Though, who am I kidding? I always feel that way. One summer a teenager jumped off the highest cliff, hit a tree coming down, and broke his neck. I remember the ambulance speeding back there. I never saw that deep, deep pool of green water the same way.

Like the kids, the dogs lived more freely back then, too. We didn't have fenced-in yards or invisible fences. Though we did our best to keep them close, the dogs were free to roam. Carmella would regularly lope off to the local dumpster, while little-legged Agatha would usually just cross the small, quiet street to the beach to watch us swim and foolishly antagonize swans. But one day, even at the periphery of the Compound, as we called the Ellses' property, we couldn't find her. A big rainstorm hit and she was gone. I paced the street for what seemed like hours but was more likely fifteen minutes, tops, calling her, my clothes soaked through completely. I didn't care. That was the first time I really thought about losing her, what shape her absence would take. I actually played it out this time. I let myself believe that she was dead and forced myself to look in the bloated high-tide creek behind our house, certain she had drowned. I stared into the bubbling marsh grass and cried.

"Found her!" I suddenly heard.

I don't remember if it was my mom or my dad, but she'd wandered three houses down to our friends Sandy and Charles's house. She'd shown up there and been given a biscuit. What better way to wait out a storm?

The feelings I was trying not to feel were starting to take a toll. After that day, I never looked at Agatha with quite the same innocence. I still loved her and held her and felt less like a human and more like an animal with her; I willingly gambled my heart for more Agatha every day. But I also eyed her more warily, like she'd betrayed me, and that was all the proof I needed to know that one day she'd betray me forever. But I was, secretly, starting to betray her, too. While Agatha and Our World remained beloved and essential, I'd begun to accommodate the increasing distractions and detritus associated with the calendar's inevitable ticking off of age; I was developing a nagging interest in a ripped, pickled *other* universe—Boy World.

Thomas was one year older and I guess we were going out, meaning we never talked but atmospherically belonged to each other. Because he was moving to London in a month, I'd agreed to kiss him. His people had convinced my people that I should just go ahead and get it over with. Thomas gave Freddie a note, who gave it to Harriet, who gave it to me, and I read it to Agatha. It was a multiple-choice questionnaire.

To: Chloe
From: Thomas

   1. Do you think I'm:

      A) Ugly

      B) Sort of cute

      C) Very cute

      D) Gorgeous

   2. Do you:

      A) Hate me

      B) Sort of like me

      C) Really like me

      D) Love me

   3. Do you want to kiss me:

      A) Never

      B) Sometime

C) Anytime

D) Now

4. Do you want to kiss me on the (check one):

❏ Cheek

❏ Lips

The reverberations of the word *kiss* made it feel like I was walking around with a bomb. Just the word sat in my stomach like a catfish for a week. I felt certain Agatha could smell that word on me. But then Freddie checked in with Harriet to see if I was going to write back, so I got to work circling all the D's and checking "cheek."

Thomas's parents were friends of my parents, and so a good-bye dinner was planned. The two of us ate early—Burger King out of paper bags in gold crowns—after which we were to disappear upstairs before the adult feast was served. I wanted to stay with the grown-ups. I always did. I knew better how to *grown-up* than *kid*, much like how Agatha seemed to know better how to *human* than *dog*. The pair of us had long discovered who the grown-ups wanted us to be, and we were good at being it. Kids and dogs, on the other hand, were terrifying. There was no telling what or who to be with them. *Lord of the Flies* and *Call of the Wild* resonate for a reason. I also knew exactly whose lips were waiting upstairs. But I couldn't make a whole *thing* out of it. Back then I didn't make whole things.

Instead, I waved to Thomas's mother and got-going-young-lady on the stairs. I could hear our parents carrying on together, their tinny voices a kind of lifeline the way my parents' dinner parties were as I fell asleep upstairs. But this was different. The promise of a kiss was involved. I shriveled with the cigared heart of leaving that world for the next one, all the dreadful human-ness waiting upstairs.

In his bedroom, I paced. I told him I needed time to think. He said *okay* and turned up Glenn Frey's "The Heat Is On," with a little goofy dancing, momentarily lightening the mood. He was very funny, this boy, which is the reason I liked him but not the reason I wanted to kiss him. The reason I wanted to kiss him was to shut everybody up and get back to Agatha. Despite what my questionnaire said, I didn't love him, but I liked him. He was someone whose eyes I blushingly met pew-over-pew during Christmas candlelight services. He was someone I always wanted to make laugh the way he made me laugh. But why did liking have to mean kissing? Couldn't we just walk like horses together? I didn't understand.

I told him that I needed to be alone for a minute, I needed time to prepare, so he showed me the room next to his, which had books and a couch and possibly a TV, but even better, a dog. Thomas's dog, Topsy, scraggled around me, offering no way out but her hot, wiry hair. I paced, Topsy paced, until Thomas checked on us. "Soon," I said, smiling. "I'm getting there." But what I was actually doing was thinking up all the tall, booming things that could prevent time from moving forward. Where were all the clunky carnivorous dinosaurs when I needed them? Where was Agatha and her varminty expression? I could not hear or see her but imagined what was possible the way Stefano Bolognini can only imagine the sound the giant Caucasian sheepdog makes: "Who knows what monstrous howls broke the long silences of the upland nights?" *Who knows.*

When I finally walked into his room, I didn't know who I

was. I'd already left my body. I was home on my boat bed, rescuing drowning animals with my boat-bed dog.

"Ready," I said like a slug might say things.

What is this ribbed system of wants here, Dog? How can a girl and a boy be so different? I don't want to be here. I don't want to be anywhere but inside the deep velvet longing of your nose. What is a kiss to you? Oh, dear Dog, do you not want them either?

Here we go, cookie: *peck!*

After the box was checked, the cheek kissed, he said, "Now you wanna do it on the lips?"

Violently on the inside, I knew my answer, but my feelings came up into my throat and stopped there like a whale on a rock.

"I need another minute," I told him, returning to the pump-up room again, but not for nearly as long.

"Okay," I said.

I bravely, barely made contact. It felt like I'd kissed the little clay worms from my pottery farm.

I sat with Agatha on my bed that night. Did she know? Did I look different? Smell different? What *do* shame and relief smell like? I kissed her between the eyes and made my lips mine again. *Hers.* My body, too. When it was just us, I didn't have to be the dog. When it was just us, I got to be the human—the girl who'd never been kissed by anyone but her dog. How much we could say to each other with our vastly different bodies, forehead-to-forehead, hand-to-paw. It was something about those long eyebrow tufts that made her look worried when I spoke aloud in full sentences. Her eyes would shift back and forth, and so would the clumps of hair. She wasn't a great keeper of eye contact, preferring a gentle hand to her body instead. And so I learned that gentle, careful touch. I read her body the way I wanted mine read.

I grazed her shorn back lightly, tickled my fingers under her red collar. I brushed her skirt of salt and pepper. Then I turned on Cyndi Lauper's "True Colors" and sang it in front of my mirror watching my face until it cried.

In the reflection behind me, Agatha was asleep on the bed. Whatever she was dreaming, she knew. A dog knows. Writes the poet Tim Seibles, "Dogs know stuff about things."

January 28, 1986. Our teacher rolled the TV into the classroom for liftoff. The *Challenger*, but most important, Christa McAuliffe, was to whiz like a big, fizzy grin into space. The whole world was waiting. We'd been following this story for years, even writing nomination letters on behalf of our substitute teacher, Elliot, the year before when he'd had no lesson plan that day— though it must be said that nominating Elliot for the role of civilian astronaut was akin to nominating Pee-wee Herman. Then, of course, we got to know the whole crew. I did, anyway. I was particularly fond of Greg Jarvis's smile and Judith Resnik's hair. But no one radiated like Christa.

Always more of an arts-and-words girl than a science-and-math one, I was absolutely mesmerized by space, by the infinite, incomprehensible black sparkle of it, and why anyone, especially a regular person, a person I might have known, would choose to go up into it. Christa could have been *my* teacher, *my* mother, *my* radical, curly-haired friend. She could have been *me*. Which was the point, I suppose. *If I can do this, kiddos, so can you.*

When the shuttle exploded and the world went to snow, our teacher didn't immediately turn the TV off—she must have been in shock, too—so we saw the torn sky and all the confused, gasping faces of the family members gathered underneath. We heard the warbled voices. *Major malfunction* are words I remember from that day. We watched the smoke trails curl out snaillike into two antennae searching for an end.

I must have known that Agatha didn't have the TV on at home, but in my mind, I zoomed right to her. It was the only way I knew how to feel held from afar. Whether we were together or not, everything that happened to me *had* to have happened to her. I needed her to share the burden of a world that always seemed to ask too much. I felt too old to cry over this in front of my friends, so, sitting on the cold, dark floor of the classroom, I coiled up inside my Agatha mind. A dog can't cry but can still feel broken. I summoned her eternal eyes and heat and zipped it all up like a sleeping bag around me. I knew in that smoking moment that she knew everything I knew, that the world was horrible and that we were together in it. When I did finally cry, I cried for us both.

Aside from writing to President Reagan at the suggestion of my mother, and receiving a letter back a few months later (how exciting it was to receive an envelope whose return address simply said: "The White House"), I don't remember otherwise processing the catastrophe that undoubtedly shattered some small melon of incorruptibility in me. I just remember moving forward with an uneasy feeling inside. It split open a certain safety and left me feeling a touch more at the mercy of the pain and inevitability of growth at the same time as I wanted nothing more than to stay inside my homegrown snow globe with Agatha. Life was a fortune, and it was a horror, too. As graceful as it was grotesque. I walked through my early field-trip days, still hoping for that magic static of brushing a particular boy's arm in the dark, blotchy turquoise of the Coney Island aquarium, but as I grew, these moments were just as likely to be the ones in which we all took turns making nonchalant, nauseating rounds at the feet end of a resting, off-duty teacher on middle school Beach Day because, rumor had it, due to a loose suit, at a certain angle, his testicle sac was visible, and that rumor was true. A peach jellyfish of opacity oozed loose. I'm not even sure if it was safety that felt diminished or innocence. That famously bitter morning of January 28, 1986—the one that cracked the O-rings that led to the fire—feels like the last morning I woke up as a kid. I was only eleven. But I felt more alone than ever. There was no Christa to believe in anymore. I felt like no matter what I did, some impossible part of my living on Earth was now up to me. When I asked her if this was true, even the dog said nothing.

I don't believe in God, Dog, but is God the thing that keeps us here, leaning into the peonies like there might be miracles inside them? You are quiet, Dog. Why? Is God the thing that hears us, or are you?

One day amid this dreadfully disillusioning year, my mother welcomed me home from school with a big yellow pad of paper.

"I thought you might have some questions about sex," she told me as Agatha jumped up and down against my shins, smelling everything my jeans had been up to that day.

That fox all up in my throat now.

It was the week my school had set aside for sex ed, and I'd already endured the traumatic demonstration of a condom being rolled onto a cucumber only to immediately pop back off and fly through the air, fluttering to the floor like a balloon several weeks after a party.

"Umm . . ."

"I thought you might have been too embarrassed to ask questions at school. Maybe you could write anything down you want to know and I'll write the answers back."

Even the can't-even seventh-grader could feel the big mama heart here. So I sat numbly at the dining room table as my mom slid a place mat under the pad to protect the dark lacquered finish of the wood from the pen. Agatha sat under the table near my feet, as she always did until—if we were eating—we told her: *Go to your pillow.* I didn't want my stout little bodyguard to go anywhere. I tugged her collar and brought her closer so I could feel the musky love, the trusty little other-body that might get me out of this. I ducked my head under the table and even *her* face seemed to say: *Fuck!* I had to come up with *something.* I heard my mom being busy around the corner in the kitchen as if doing sound effects for a radio show. Cue the cabinets opening and closing! Cue the cracking of the ice trays! Cue the burner going click-click-click! I had to come up with *something* before she was full of eyes back in here.

What are the things I know, Dog? What are the things I don't know?

There were the games of spin the bottle and truth or dare that I never dared play, only watched from the sidelines with Harriet. (*Prudes*, we were called. *Lesbians.*) And there were the weird things I'd heard that could happen in the closet during those games: hands on boobs, mouths on penises. There was the older girl who, rumor had it, had gotten an abortion, whatever an abortion had to do with an actual baby inside an actual body. And there was the student smoking lounge (you heard me), which my friends and I periodically dared each other to run past all the way through lower middle school. That seemed to have something to do with sex. Right? Tattoos, Mohawks, leather. Could any of those make you pregnant? There was liking boys but not want-ing to touch them, not wanting to be touched. There was being touched anyway. There was the *Joy of Sex* book I'd snuck through just for all those wispy illustrations of ecstasy, whatever ecstasy was. There was the sex hotline, those strange, creaturely promises on the other end. And the R-rated movie my friend's babysit-ter played for us at her third-grade birthday sleepover—a full, wet penis in the shower! (My mom called the parents after that one.) All of these details seemed to dangle like uncomfortable ornaments before the more sweeping backdrop of a generally sexualized school environment and the constant rumors (now, investigations have shown, not just rumors) about teachers and students being sexually involved. I never spoke of this at home, of course, but by seventh grade I already held the names of some of those rumored teachers and students like they were a handful of lollipops I'd snuck home in my bag. I didn't know anything. I knew way too much.

"Okay!" I finally said, a little chirp. "I wrote one."

"Great!" my mother sang back, practically skipping in.

She returned to the table and I slid the pad over, looking up, down, then forever into the black square of the place mat as she read my question silently: *Why is a blow job called a blow job?*

Understandably having expected something more along the lines of, *So, like, how exactly are babies made again?* she worked hard to adjust her face. After a few earnest seconds, she let out a laugh that felt like it had been stuck for too long.

"I have no idea!" she yelled, making me let out a laugh that had been stuck for too long, too. We startled Agatha, which suddenly made her very much the dog here. Our shared human moment seemed briefly to cut through the girl-canine spell Agatha and I had so observantly cast. But it didn't last long. The staccato clacking of her nails on the hardwood floor sounded like a typewriter, like a small, combustible thing full of words, and I gratefully fell back into her graces.

She's a whole system of stars sitting here, Dog. Is this what it feels like to be human? This sitting and staying and being and feeling? This aorta-to-aorta diving in? It feels weird. And by weird, *I might mean* good. *If I could feel anything. If I could sit. If I could stay.*

Back up in our room, Agatha lay on my rug with her head down and her eyes open, her eyebrow whiskers flicking back and forth like she was trying not to look at me. Had everything just changed? Had she heard something that made me a little gross now, a little *too* human? I sat on the rug next to her and gently placed my hand on the back of her neck. She often rolled onto her back when I did this, offering me her pink-gray piggy belly, but not this time. This time, she just froze. I tickled around her collar. She kept her chin to the shag as if hoping I'd get busy with something else. As if it were now up to me to shift this uncomfortable canyon that ultimately, undeniably, divided us into two separate species. *Be the human,* I swear I heard her broken heart say.

There is something so bewitching about a city dog, something simultaneously unnatural and at ease. If you want to fully appreciate how adaptable dogs are, you need not go farther than your nearest city and watch them methodically pee on pavement, blithely canter under their doggie umbrellas, and ride public transportation inside tote bags. Having grown up in the city with city dogs and now living in the country with country dogs, I truly marvel at the difference. They are like two entirely different species. As with its vigorous people and sartorial sway, if I stay away too long, I return to the Big Apple a bit unpracticed and intimidated, even by the dogs. As I bob along the sidewalks like an escaped chicken, the dogs around me trot as sure-footed as swans. The pugs possess a more confident gait. They pass me without acknowledgment or expression, like even they know they don't have time for me. They are as erudite and persistent as their people. While wandering the carpet of hexagonals on the Promenade, I swear I once saw a King Charles spaniel filling out the crossword puzzle in the *New York Times.* If a country dog is a wolf in a Santa hat, then a city dog might as well *be* Santa.

Agatha was unique in that she was both a city dog and a country dog. She had to adjust her wolfness not only once, but every time we packed her up and drove her back and forth between Connecticut and New York City. She's the only dog I've ever had who's owned a sweater, but you'd never catch her wearing it outside the city limits—except for once in New Hampshire when it was simply that cold. She peed with aplomb no matter the surface, squatting over curbs *and* crabapples like an Olympic gymnast. In stark contrast, whenever we brought Booker and Safari into the city with us, it took them more than twenty-four hours to pee without the requisite stimulation of grass. It's the human in me that interprets this as somehow soft—as a way in which my big, lumbering country dogs don't quite have it all together. But it's those same big, lumbering nonpee-ers on pavement who know a thing or two about bobcats and the swampy, primordial smell of the deep woods, midday.

A dog is a winning mimic. City or country, street or stream, a dog wants to be you, even when you don't want to be you at all.

School was out for the day, the dogwoods and cherry blossoms wide up and roaming. I was thirteen and had the ankle-zipper jeans, self-cut wispy bangs, and heavy blue eyeliner to prove it. I cued up my Walkman. Bruce Springsteen's *Born in the USA*, Whitney Houston's *Whitney*, and the Beastie Boys' *Licensed to Ill* had been in heavy rotation. That day, it was the Beasties, and I was kicking it live past the Unitarian church and all the high schoolers smoking and making out on the dark, low stairs.

The music occupied only the very center of my hearing. All around the periphery was Brooklyn, Brooklyn-ing. People, pigeons, delivery trucks, truth. And a pack of seventh-grade boys coming up from behind. I heard them laugh, so I turned to see who and my stomach went up on my head like a hat. Five of them, maybe six. Two I considered friends. The rest were the ones who scared me, the ones who acted older, talked older, smoked pot, who called me prude and flat and lesbian. They were getting closer and I felt panicked, sick. I could say hi. Or just ignore them, get lost in the music somewhere. That could be cool, to be so cool. But they might mistake cool for mean, and I'm not mean, I'm nice. I'm a person who says hi. *Just say hi. It's easier to say hi. Smile. Be nice.*

But before I could be anything, a hand was on my ass. The first hand that had ever been there, aside from my mother's and father's back when they were changing my diapers. I was a baby then. I wasn't a baby anymore. I'd kissed a couple of boys, held a few hands, pressed my knee into someone else's knee on the field-trip bus, and that was it. I'd had crushes, "gone out" with a few boys. I'd square-danced with Pando at summer camp under the barn roof pelted with rain in a panda sweater vest my grandmother had knit for me. But I'd yet to have a real boyfriend. I'd yet to want one.

So I went dead inside as the hand—attached to the biggest boy, the one I feared the most—squeezed and shoved and pushed my body around. The hand felt like it must have been under my jeans (it wasn't), because it was touching more than just my buttock. And now he was using both hands. It was hard to know or feel or do anything, except the one time I turned my head to see what my two friends were doing: laughing with the rest. They didn't look at me, but at each other, nostrils fanning like panicked bunnies, proving they were game. I never stopped walking, even with the boy's hands clinging to me like an angry *Architeuthis* as the others instinctively made a kind of horseshoe formation around me.

I knew enough to know that whatever this was, whatever this was going to be, I didn't want to be there for it, so I floated up and away, leaving the street boys and the Beastie Boys all strung up below inside a cloud of spring and slang and grope and laughter. I didn't know where I was, but I was gone—high up in the quick ash of *Challenger* dust with Christa, laid flat atop a whale at the farthest-out point of the sea—and I wasn't coming back until it was over. I went gray, scraping the soft, hazy steepness of my body without me. I couldn't go dog here. Nothing could hold me in this. All I was, was not there.

The big boy made a hungry munch-munch sound with one last deep squeeze between my legs, then he let me go. He howled into the sky and they all walked ahead, sticking close like a pack of wolves after a kill. I could still hear the sound of their laughter half a block away, though it wasn't the big boy laughing, it was the others as they gathered around him, propping him up, I imagine fearing him, too. No one, not even my friends, ever turned around to look at me. If they had, they would have seen that although I couldn't feel my legs, they were still walking—they'd never stopped walking. I did my best after to look exactly as I had before, getting ahold of my frantic heart as if strangling a bird with my hands. That way nobody would know anything—not my parents, not my friends, not even my dog. For once I was holding on to something I didn't want even Agatha to know. When she saw me coming, I wanted to be the girl—*her* girl—still kicking it live to the music, the girl who'd never been touched on her ass by another human hand, aside from her mother's and father's back when they were changing her diapers.

What next, Dog? I remember thinking. *Was that rape? Whatever rape is, other than a word I heard someone say on the back stairs one day. Is this upsetting to you, Dog? Is it funny? What does a hand on an ass mean—and why?*

I've always wondered if anyone saw this happen. Out on the street, one block from my school, three blocks from my home, in the beautiful, long, golden light of late day. I've wondered if anyone saw a swarm of boys pass too roughly through a girl; a girl, violated. I've wondered if anyone watching was thinking the same as me: How far will they take this? And if they saw what happened and still decided how far it got was not too far. Did it look fun from a distance? Did I look happy as I darkly left my body to fend for itself? Did I look fine? It seems impossible that nobody saw—a law student headed to the courthouse around the corner? Another schoolmate? It was a busy street, especially when school let out around three. But, no one. No one broke it up. No one asked if I was all right. No one put their body in front of my body at the terrifying uncertainty of what could come next, of all that had already transpired.

None of my humans were home when I got there. Only wiggling, hopping, squealing Agatha, who was ready for her walk, ready for me. But I wasn't ready to walk her. The big boy lived around the corner and I sure didn't want to run into him. Though what would that have been like for him to encounter me alone, no pack hunkered in around him, no terrified sidekicks, no cheerleaders? I sat with Agatha on the window seat in the living room and watched for him, his unmistakable towering, bumpy stride and flopping flap of hair. I pulled her in so close until we practically merged bodies, until I could feel less of it all, until she again could hold these terrible bits of me. When it seemed safe, I took her to the Promenade, holding the leash like it was my own hand, moving my body away from those moments that had taken *me* from me. I did what always brought only comfort. I walked my little dog and my little dog walked me.

Josh was a senior; I was a freshman. It was not so long ago that I had been rolling the hills of Treetops, learning how to boil an egg, getting my first period, standing in solidarity with Harriet on the perplexing, consequential periphery of spin the bottle. It was not so long ago that I had remained rooted in my life as part dog. Agatha hadn't understood either the point of kissing a boy, and so in this, too, we'd bunked up and settled in. But in that way bodies eventually take you over, tell you what you want, who you are, the way even the most dog of humans can't forever be dog, mine suddenly buckled at the sight of him. In a sudden, brazen burst, I felt certain I could love this boy, whatever loving a boy was. This was the boy with whom, for whom, I wanted to find out—this boy of red hair and brown eyes and easy smiles, this boy I had yet to talk to, this boy whose arrival meant only one thing: making room for a boy where there had only been room for Agatha. Since our age difference meant it was never going to happen, I decided what's the harm in just getting the word out, openly having a crush on this beautiful, untouchable boy. So I started talking to people other than Agatha about him. I told anyone who would listen that I thought Josh was hot—though fourteen-year-old me probably used the word *cute* or *adorable*. I even mentioned it to my photography teacher, who was also his photography teacher, in the hopes that she might tell him. I developed a habit of writing his name everywhere—notebooks, desks, the inside of my arm once, just in case someone, Josh, maybe, or God, if there is a God, was watching.

He looks so friendly when he laughs, Dog. I wish I had boobs big enough to be called boobs, not "soft pennies," like my doctor called the stage I'm in. Maybe I'll just hold my books in front of my chest all the time. But I'm at school. Have you ever seen someone walk without moving their hands, Dog? Even weirder than no boobs.

One midwinter's day in 1990, I pushed the eighth-floor door to the stairs open, quick, quick double-stepping down to class, and suddenly there was Josh, quick hop-stepping up the stairs past me. We were the only two living creatures on Earth.

"Hi, Chloe," he said, like a friendly balloon just hovering there for a minute before floating up.

"Hi, Josh," I said back, no big whoop.

But I felt like a flying hubcap. *I'm a name now, Dog.* I found the nearest bathroom to wait for my blushing to end. I was ten minutes late to class.

Then I was a first date. In early February, in the middle of the school lobby, Josh asked me out to lunch. And on Friday, February 9, we went to Teresa's, a Polish restaurant a few blocks from school. Chicken noodle soup was all my love-struck stomach could handle. At the end of the meal, I slid the napkin I'd used into my pocket so that at age forty-three, I could find it wrapped in a twenty-nine-year-old rubber band inside a red and black shoebox on what my mother now refers to as the Top Shelf, as in "You've got to do something about *the Top Shelf*," meaning the top shelf of my childhood closet where my history of boys still lies.

We kissed with our tongues during Driving Miss Daisy, *Dog! It rained on us the whole way home!*

Outside the house on Pierrepont Street that had raised me from a puppy, Josh and I stood under his umbrella and kissed until our feet were soaking and I didn't care who in the world could see us, even Agatha, who might have been watching from our window seat, for all I knew, waiting for me the way I would soon be waiting for Josh, gazing out the window for signs of serendipity and fate.

In the fall of 1990, Josh and my heart headed to Princeton. It took several trains to get there but only a few hours total. Still, between high school and college burned a whole world. Though I didn't see it that way. My love with Josh was so strong I felt sure sophomore-in-high-school had a natural home in campus life. I wasn't allowed to spend the night for that first year, which felt terribly unfair to me (the now-parent in me must gently remind you—or myself—that I was *fifteen*). I never got as far as actually proposing this out loud, but I did decide the only way I could safely stay the night was by taking Agatha with me. *She* could be the dog that went everywhere and met everyone, the way I'd imagined Agatha 1 would be. *We* could be the Dog and the Girl. *She* would choose my husband for me, hold out her thick little paw and cry, *"Him!"*

But no. I was only allowed to visit for the day. I'd arrive midmorning to his roommates blasting "Cradle of Love" and head home to Agatha early evening, just as all the parties were getting underway.

Once back at home, I pined as if Josh were at war. I sulked around, heartsick, spending all of my free time writing him letters, baking him cookies, pickling myself in the deep, reverent pain of a full and lonely heart that Agatha could only momentarily relieve. I never could have put this feeling into words then, but while she was still company in my adolescent suffering, Agatha was already less a solution to it. She was steady and without judgment. She was everything the torment of human love was *not*. She was grace and peace, as described by Milan Kundera: "Dogs are our link to paradise. They don't know evil or jealousy or discontent. To sit with a dog on a hillside on a glorious afternoon is to be back in Eden, where doing nothing was not boring—it was peace." Agatha was peace. And sometimes peace isn't even enough.

I was almost sixteen when Josh and I first tried sex, before I'd ever used a tampon. We'd spent a year and a half high up in the air, reveling in our soaring, sweet love of one another like ravens working the thermals over a canyon. His body was the second body I'd ever known, next to my own, and I was still getting to know my own. I even knew Agatha's better just from grooming her, holding her, sleeping with her, her taut, bristly back snug up against my smooth stomach. Sex hurt, which I knew it was supposed to at first, but something wasn't working. So I bought a box of tampons before one of our weekend trips to his parents' house on Long Island because I remembered the little diagram showing what the inside of me looked like, and hopefully, then, what should go where. And as I remember Josh now and what a strange, magnificent system it is to know your *first person*, to be known, this might be my dearest image of him—of us: we are sitting in his bed together and, in the light of a single table lamp, studying the diagram, holding hands.

In the middle of my senior year of high school, the vet found a tumor the size of a grapefruit inside Agatha's abdomen—a giant for such a little dog. She must have had symptoms for him to go in and look, but I don't remember what they were. She was twelve now, an undeniable senior. She had grayed and slowed, but she was a tough-cookie terrier—the Diehard, after all. She still found sun where she could. She still chased Pearl the cat when provoked. She still looked back at us from under her crazy, party-favor eyebrows, as if saying, *Why is everybody looking at me with tumors in their eyes?* The vet gave us a surgical option to remove it and so that's what we did. The surgery went well and so did her recovery, but the feeling in my own abdomen that sprang up at the first mention of the word *tumor* felt like it had formed a tumor in and of itself. It was like the sudden, next stage after losing her in the rainstorm years before. She had one more paw in the grave. And there was no imagining a life—or a *Me*—without her. But for the 90 percent of my heart that was already, as a precaution, shattered, there was 10 percent still holding out for the possibility that she might be the first dog to live forever.

I trod carefully that last year of high school, taking her for extra walks along the curb all the way down to the Promenade to see what boats were afloat that day. I lay with her in my bed longer, settling in for Forehead Time (though now I had Josh's forehead, too). We would lie together, face-to-face, our nose slopes and foreheads fitting perfectly (now I fit perfectly with Josh, too). Our eyes were so close, the whole world was gone (Josh could make the whole world go away, too). I walked her to school one late afternoon and held her in my arms for my senior yearbook photo. She was the first dog I loved more than myself. The dog who saw all the things, heard all the things, knew all the things I could be when it was just the two of us batting about in that vivid, carnivorous arena where we were never wholly human, never wholly dog, but some magnificent super-species between. If we couldn't be that anymore, where did that leave us? Though I'd been on this trajectory for a while now, often choosing Josh Time over Agatha Time, I started becoming more aware of the finality of this choice—that every time I chose him over her was another moment with her blinked away. With Dog no longer as my witness, what would it mean to be the dog now? To be *me*?

As Agatha recovered and reassured us with her late-in-life second wind, late that spring of 1993, the same week as my high school graduation, Josh's mother, Ina, was diagnosed with ovarian cancer. Though it's sometimes hard to make room for any other characters when playing out the scenes of a first love, or a first dog—it looks as it feels: as if the rest of the world has dropped away. I don't think any of our parents were initially thrilled about our age difference, or, perhaps, about the intensity of our commitment at such tender ages, but that all seemed to dissipate quickly as everyone got to know each other and a deep mutual affection between our families was made—the deepest, I think, between Ina and me.

For all that could go unsaid in my home, everything in Josh's was loud and clear. There were no resident animals in which to hide. At first, there was a lot I didn't say because I thought I shouldn't, because—for reasons of nature, nurture, both—I *couldn't*. My earliest memories of my time with his family are of nervously sitting at the dining room table, blushing persistently, privately hoping no one other than Josh would look my way. But I got over that pretty quickly. Loving and feeling loved will do that. So will feeling known. Ina especially (and Josh, of course) made me feel both. Her propensity to say real things made me feel real, made me feel known, even if that feeling also sometimes jarred me.

After an initial surgery, she was put on a heavy course of chemotherapy. A lot of that summer was spent visiting by her bed when she was up for visitors, which she wasn't always, in which case we planned meals and waited for what was next in the quiet. Sometimes I'd lie next to her while Josh would entertain us. Sometimes we'd take turns quietly talking with her when she didn't feel well enough to sit up. We all just wanted to bring out her fluorescent smile. We wanted to make her better. Instead, she lost her hair. I brought her a stuffed cat one day because my mom always brought me stuffed animals when I was sick. Of course, I'd had the flu; she had cancer. What I really wanted to do was bring her Agatha, but she was not entirely herself either. She was more tired, more slow. Unbeknownst to us, she was at war again with a tumor of her own. Nothing I could do that summer could get rid of the sick or the look of the sick, at Josh's house or my own. I started having the sensation of floating again, of being outside my body, of departing all that was emerald and real for the soft, winded gray of escape. Though where exactly was I? The dog I'd always been was fading. *Agatha* was fading. There was too much tumor in her to make room for me anymore. My mother-away-from-home was fading, too. I sat suspended. Blank-minded and bare, I hovered somewhere up near the sun.

What's the difference between the dead and the living, Dog? Is there anything earnest to learn when tumors grow? How can I feel so safe with you and yet like I still know nothing about life on Earth? Are you telling me something more vital like I've always believed? Are you just simply amused by my breath? How am I ever to know?

Then, on August 5, 1993, like Icarus, but with wings of dog hair, I crashed back down on our deck, where Agatha lay, belly bloated, unable to stand. All she could do was stare out from eyes with nobody in them.

Our vet at the time was in Connecticut, so my mom planned to drive her there. I don't remember if anyone asked me if

I wanted to go, or suggested that I go, but I immediately knew I wanted nothing to do with it. It was too overwhelming, too scary, too hard, too *real*. At the same time, I knew that when my mom took her to the car, the same thing would happen that always happened when my mom took dogs to the car: I'd never see her again. We didn't say that, of course. On the surface, everything we did tried to convey the possibility that she might live. But we all knew. She seemed a little dead already, lying outside on our deck where we'd hoped she would at least appreciate the fresh air. And so that is where she was when I kissed her for the last time, felt the warm, fuzzy slope between her eyes, the place I always went to learn things, to know things, to know how to be *me*—and how *not* to be me. How to give *me* to someone else to hold for a while. The only place on Earth where I loved myself truly: in the brine of her twinkling-grape nose. I told her I loved her, as if that would mean something to her other than *throat, tongue, air*, and left for my summer job as a receptionist at my dad's office on University and Eleventh, leaving behind in Brooklyn all that was booming and dying.

"Beyer Blinder Belle?" I said in my professional singsong from my receptionist chair, hours later.

"Hi, honey," my mom said, her voice dropping. "She's gone."

Then she did what she needed to do to get through it herself. She dove into the details about how the tumor had grown back and burst and the reason she was bloated is she was bleeding internally, also indicated by her pale gums. She got talking so hard there wasn't room for anything else. I hung up. I was too filled up with my own emotional stockpile to take anything in. It would be decades before I even formed the thought that that must have been such a hard day for her, driving our dear dog—

our dog of one million magnificent things!—to her death. Being her One Person, the last woman standing, at the end.

I ran for the subway home. A couple of blocks down Broadway, I heard, "Chloe! Chloe!" I turned and fell smack into my dad's chest. He'd had to run to catch me. He held me there in the middle of the summer city. "I'm so sorry . . . ," he kept saying. "It's so sad. . . ." I couldn't talk, I only sobbed into his perfectly starched button-down, told him I had to go home, and wearily made my way down into the sweltering dark of the station, where I hid in the forgiving anonymity of the multitudes.

I lay on the couch and cried for what seemed like weeks. Friends and neighbors called, leaving messages on the answering machine. I never picked up. It was even impossible to talk to Harriet and Josh. There was only one person I did grief with, and that was Agatha. So I watched soap operas for the first time in my life and cried and cried and cried. Eventually, I had to go back to work; my boss-dad was kind to let me wallow for a while but probably also recognized the importance of getting back on my feet—which I was only able to do by not talking about Agatha, making it clear I didn't want to talk about Agatha if anyone tried. I went silent. I went inside. For thirteen years, she had been the emotional center of a family who, when they weren't sure how to look at each other, looked at each other through the dog.

Josh spent the night at my house before the morning my parents drove me to college. I remember waving to him as he stood on our stoop. We were both crying. I was crying for who was left there (Josh) and for who wasn't there anymore (Agatha). Instead of her warm body, I held a watermelon of air in my lap as I caught the last glimpse of Josh's wet face as we drove up

Pierrepont toward Williams College. I already knew I was too scared to be with him anymore, same as I knew I was too scared to be without my dog. I couldn't accompany her the way she'd accompanied me—I was too human. I couldn't accompany Josh either—I was too dog.

A few weeks later, I broke up with Josh, just days into my freshman year. It's taken me more than twenty years to see it, but I ended that relationship because I wanted to leave everything about home and that summer behind. Even if that meant Josh. Josh now came with a dying mother, and Ina's illness, the possibility of losing her, was not something I was equipped to handle. I survived the summer partially on the belief that though the days were hard, everything would be okay—everything would be *fine*. This would one day be a story to tell, not a bereavement to endure. I was not acknowledging where we all were and sitting there in it. I didn't know how. Before that shocking, spectacular feeling of being known could be taken from me, I pushed the Known and the Loved away. I walked like a horse as fast as I could in the opposite direction.

No longer could I shrink myself deep into the carefully strung chambers of Agatha's atomic heart. Its beat was gone, unable to contain me. Instead, I wore her name tag around my neck. For years, I would hear songs from that wretched summer—in the car, in stores—and my eyes would fill with all I'd loved, all I'd lost, all I'd worked so hard to avoid about the impossible death of a first dog and a first love and a second mother.

For thirteen years, the exact number of years that Agatha was alive, I would be dogless, walking like the whole herd of malignancies that took the dog from me.

A dog is the absence of things—what you get when you take the bad stuff away. Absence of fear. Absence of evil. Absence of death. A dog is a lonely heart without all the loneliness.

But the dog now *was* the absence. She *was* the death. The lonely heart with *all* the loneliness. You tell me how there could ever be another.

The Dog House

There's a ray of holy light frozen on Booker's grave. It was never part of our plan in burying him where we did, but somehow we chose a spot where both morning and evening light settles—the kind of waxing and waning light that holds something purposeful and primitive. It's the waning kind now, late afternoon, and the sun hits the gold and blue of the rock I painted with "B 2000–2015." Like a moth, I suppose, like a mother, when the grave lights up, I come. I remember everything there is to remember. Which is to say, love everything there is to love.

I lost three whole, wriggling dogs before Booker, but he's the one whose gilded entrance and exit compelled me to ask what a dog is. He's the one without whom my life would have taken a wildly different path. I had the life I had with him, and now have without him, *because* of him. I said yes to meeting a dog and along came a whole harmony of humans. And so remembering him and loving him are one and the same.

Dan Savage tells the story of his mother's death on a live episode of *This American Life* and it's the shaky, real part of his throat with which he speaks. Her last words were, "Remember me," which, every time I listen to it, I hear as "I love you." I imagine that's one thing you might fear as you're dying—that you won't be able to remember anything, you will no longer be able to hold the stories, the things you love, and therefore *love* anything anymore, so you might ask to be remembered instead, to be held, loved as a way of remembering and continuing to love yourself. *I want to stay with you. I want to love you. I want to remember you. But I fear I can't. Remember me.*

That's what we were all doing there on Saranac Lake earlier this summer. We were remembering my husband's aunt Margo before she was gone. At that same annual family reunion last year, she'd received a call from her doctor delivering the diagnosis of liver cancer, stage IV. She was given six to nine months, but one year later, she was still here—a little weak and tired from the chemo, but holding steady, living and loving with cancer in quite a becoming blond-gray wig.

It was loon-dark. Some were making s'mores at the campfire. A dozen kids ran wild through the moonlight, and we all sent out the impulsive hope that they were looking out for each other. The Shaw clan, as we often call the family I married into, is a family of big loving and living. And like Josh's family did so many years ago, the Shaws initially overwhelmed me. I ended my first night at my first of these reunions by myself, sobbing over all those many people outside who, simply because Matt and I had fallen in love, wanted to look me in the eye, *know* me.

I was sitting on a bench overlooking the scene with Margo—Gogo, her loved ones say. We were doing what's never come naturally to me; we were sharing some quiet together. I'd always been prone to filling quiet right up, because *God knows* what might come out of it. But I took her cue. Because she was quiet, I was quiet, too.

The first night we celebrated her seventy-fourth birthday. I was sitting next to her husband, Bob—Baba, his loved ones say—before they brought out the cake. He was watching as one of his granddaughters helped Margo figure something out on her phone.

"I should take pictures," he said to no one in particular, or to himself, standing to capture the moment on film.

Remember me.

When her cake was brought out, everyone whipped out a phone. Her eyes were wet. Our eyes were wet. Her last birthday. Or would it be? We'd thought last year was her last.

Margo's grandson Chapman walked over for a snuggle and to make sure he and she would be on the same team for golf the next morning.

"Of *course*," she said, hugging him.

"Yesssss," he said with a casual fist pump, pushing back off into Cousinland.

Remember me.

The visitation shifted something in the atmosphere and we began to talk—about child-rearing, elementary schools, writing, cooking, dogs. I'm not sure she's ever been a dog person, but she always humored me in listening to me talk about mine. It was clear from the beginning that she knew me, she'd listened: years ago, for our engagement, she and Bob gave us a glass paperweight of two dogs lying together, curled around each other, neck-in-neck. It's what I use as a place-keeper when writing.

That night, she was wrapped in a gray cashmere blanket that she pulled in tighter as the sky got darker.

"That's a beautiful blanket," I said, rubbing the soft gray yarn between my finger and thumb.

"Isn't it though?" Margo said. "Bob gave it to me for Christmas. It's really a better wrap than blanket, but if you have a husband like mine who will tuck it beneath your feet when you lie down, it's the perfect blanket."

Remember me.

Back inside, I boil a few batches of sugar water for the hummingbirds and fill the two feeders, one on either side of the house. The weather has been so beautiful for so many days, which means I'm longing for a good storm—a longing that is never guilt-free. On the very long list of things Safari is afraid of, storms rank as number one. What's funny to me now is that fear of storms may be one of the essential life lessons Booker taught Safari, along with walking on a leash and finding the cool kitchen tile during heat waves. Booker was terrified of storms— and firecrackers. We always found him in the bathtub. I love imagining that at the beginning, Safari was afraid of everything *but* storms—and firecrackers—but when he saw Booker head for the tub he lost his shit and followed suit. Safari has always had his own beloved fear practices. At the first quiver of thunder, which he always feels before we do, he wedges himself into the most unsuitable and awkward spaces in our closets, doing his absolute weirdo best to disappear—to trade in being the dog, for God's sake, for being the closet. Finding him in one kind of knotted yoga pose or another, drooling all over the shoes, is usually how I determine how close a storm is. All of this while Otter stands in the pouring rain with *such* ease I wonder if he even knows it's raining. *What is rain?* I imagine him thinking. *Chipmunks.*

Day two in the Dog House, and, even with Safari and Otter looking at me hungry like wolves—do dogs undress you with their eyes?—I am longing for my human pack. From the pictures Matt sends me, I can tell they're all having the same spectacular sunny spell. Rae made a pal at clay camp and they're meeting up for a swim. Jackson, as usual, has become everyone's friend. When these little love missives arrive from the ether, I can't tell if I want more of them or less. I laugh out loud at a slo-mo video of Rae and Matt running off a paddleboard and jumping into the middle of the lake. I do the same at a video of Jackson and his uncle David having an "Uncle" contest: who can eat the grossest concoction of food the other made. But I could just as easily cry at all I am missing. All the life being lived without me—and without them. How to want *this* and *that*? How to feel like I can't have *that* until I endure *this*? Until I figure out how to bring all of my worlds, Dog, Girl, Woman, Wife, Mother, together. Just as Booker's life so exquisitely fused my separate selves, Booker's death left me splintered all over again. And here in the middle of my solitude, I want nothing more than to summon him, bring him—abracadabra!—into a great, feathery fireball at my feet.

Perhaps because the last time I had this kind of solitude was with that very shimmering matrix of a dog—the only dog, until this Dog House, with whom I'd ever spent such sustained isolation. In 2007, I drove Booker to my mother's family's cottage on Higgins Lake in Michigan for ten days for a similar sabbatical. Matt and Booker and I were not yet engaged. As part of a more-than-one-hundred-year-old association founded, in part, by an ancestor of mine, our cottage is one of maybe forty cottages that in the summer months share a dining hall, serving three meals a day, with the exception of Sunday dinner. The system is nothing if not Pavlovian. You eat when a bell rings. It's no wonder I'm always hungry around churches.

I've spent a week or two at Higgins nearly every summer of my life, but always in the company of grandparents, parents, friends, boyfriends, aunts, uncles, cousins, my husband and kids (rarely dogs, though—until recently, they've only been allowed off season). I'd never spent a single night alone there, and, as with most forthcoming solitude, it was the nights that, even before arriving, were giving me pause. But the dog helped. He and I spent the week defying what dogs and humans are and both became the lake.

I've come to think of it as our own honeymoon, which, given that I fell for Matt and Booker simultaneously, only seems fair; he didn't get to go to St. John with us. On the shores of Higgins Lake, we ran down the pine path together—he off-leash, me off-line. We sat in the boathouse—he at my feet, me at my desk, both of us entranced by the turquoise ripple arrangement of the lake. We broke for swims, but not before I had to teach him that this was not like Keuka Lake, a Finger Lake of western New York, the lake he'd grown up on, a deep and narrow Y-shaped stunner banked by rolling green vineyards and farms. He'd learned long before I knew him that when you see a lake, you run full speed down the dock and jump in. At the end of the Keuka dock, it's deep enough, but at the two-foot-deep end of the Higgins dock, that approach might paralyze you. So I taught him to wade in with me from shore, which was admittedly less spectacular but also less animal hospital–y. As we walked out to the deeper waters, which takes a good while, I pretended we were Alec and the Black of *The Black Stallion* in the scene when Alec coaxes the mighty, timid horse out from their island isolation into the sea so that he might more easily mount him. I pictured that entrancing, otherworldly underwater footage as our own—leg and foreleg, Woman and Animal, float-marching together, elegantly sending up small, cloudy explosions of sand.

I remember wondering that week if he thought I'd kidnapped him. Here we were, hundreds of miles away from home in a place he'd never been, and Matt was nowhere to be seen. I mean, of course he didn't think that, but did he ever wonder if this unusual situation meant something was wrong, or, like me, could he revel in, trust in, the beauty of the lake and woods and time together, the same way I wonder now if Safari and Otter, recognizing the absence of everybody else, are thinking, *Woo-hoo! We get her all to ourselves!* Do they carry around images of what or who is *not* here, or are they confined to a deeper understanding of precisely what here *is*? A beetle. A storm. A week of watching their number one lady reckon with all that has so far come. They don't feel trapped or restricted. They are alive, so they live.

Otter charges at the window screen, growl-barking in his thickest dog accent, as ever fully *him* as can be. Sometimes when he does this, there's nothing there—at least to my inferior senses.

But today there's a family of wild turkeys. Two adult turkeys and eight turkey babies, maybe turkey tweens. I've seen smaller. The tweens nibble around the back of our yard while the adults do the worrying about the growl-barking, which has mostly stopped at my request. Safari has joined us on the porch now because *something is happening, something is out there.* And now the whole turkey team shifts right and meanders beneath the play set, causing me to send up the tiny hope that at least one tween might be tempted to try out the monkey bars or slide, but also rocketing me straight into road panic, which I always slip into when wildlife heads in the direction of the road. I refuse to let a family of turkeys die on my watch.

I head out the patio door and they scramble back until I think they're far enough to have changed their minds about what's the better direction here. "There," I say aloud, satisfied. Otter's ears go banana-cakes at what this might mean. *Word! Love! Eat it!?* But they head faster now toward the road. I sit, helpless, my face in my hands, waiting for the tire screech of smushed babies. I hold my breath. I hold my breath. Then one of the adults comes running back like a person, like a full-on cross-country champ, sprinting all leggy across the lawn, back into the dead-dark of the bulky summer woods. *God*, I think. *The lone survivor.* But when I look out my husband's roadside office window, there, marching up a small hill in the field on the other side of the road, is the other adult and the content, crooked line of dutiful babies. I am no wild turkey, but this seems devastating to me. How on earth will they ever find each other again? Then it occurs to me that I am looking at my own family—one parent, parenting, while the other heads into the woods.

How did I become the one in the woods, Dog? Will the one in

*the woods be remembered, too? How? Did Easy leave with thoughts
of the Unbearable Child or a nice little hippo-toothed blanket-eater?
Did Agatha 1 find my pillow revolting or divine? Agatha 2, my fear
repetitive or sweet? Does Booker remember me as Mother or Friend? Toy
Producer or Rogue Pancake Dropper? Boot Stomper or Face Smoother?
How do I remember him?*

Booker: Dog of Marriage

(2006–2015)

While the first eighteen years of my life come back to me with a luxurious patience, a moving but meandering sense of time, I am only able to revisit the thirteen-year period of my doglessness—essentially, the decade of my twenties—in fast motion, an almost warp speed that makes it difficult to be still in any one part of it, to remember it in any full-bodied way. College whipped around me like a sandstorm. I had the sensation of so many things but could only see what was immediately before me. In that prying murk surfaced countless new methods of being the dog—being the books, being the drinks, being the love. After those potent flying-squirrel years, there were a handful of (mostly good) jobs, a handful of (mostly good) cities, a handful of (mostly good) men. I learned the difference between *wanting love* and *actually loving*, like the difference between a sea lion and a seal, one hearing through ears that remain outside the body, the other through holes punched all the way in. Easy to mistake one for the other, those brown commas of slick lard, slipping in and out of the same pool.

Through the jobs, through the cities, through the men, even, there was always Agatha's metal name tag sliding around at the bottom of my jewelry box. Every now and then, I stumbled across it while rummaging through in search of an earring backing or a long-deserted ring, and I'd hold on to it, let it sink into my hand like the deep yearning I still had for that trucky little Scottie body flopped like a fish across my lap. I'd rub the impression of her name as if it were transmitting to me something extraterrestrial as I remembered my fingers on her warm, sheared back in all the blinding heat of my third decade. I heard her calling me by the nickname dear ones always get to: *You told me what you thought of the deepest part of the ocean, Chlo. Remember, there on your bed? So many things I longed to say but couldn't. So many times you have asked what a dog is. You said, Dog, is a dog a hot-pink party balloon filled with human sorrow? I wish you could have heard me when I grumbled, No, then, Yes! I am part of the ocean now, too— bubbling, that horrific kind of blue. Not here, but everywhere. Even without my nose, I can see you. Without my legs, I can walk with you. Without me, though, you have to feel yourself around. You have to feel.*

In the spring of 2006, the relationship I was in came to a startling end. It was no doubt for the best, but the man I'd been dating for more than a year, the man who'd just recently moved into my apartment, woke up in an agitated state one morning, walked out of that apartment, and I never saw him again. It was a disturbing enough cap to the tumultuous decade of my twenties that I swore off men. Bucking all stereotypes of lonely-hearted single women in their twenties, I adopted a cat—my second, Lolita. My first cat, Tito, had been adopted after the previous breakup. I'd never loved cats the way I loved dogs, so it's funny to me that it never once occurred to me to adopt a dog. A cat just seemed easier, more practical—and the landlords were thrilled at the idea since, like every building in the city, this one housed an undeniable rodent population. As Robert Sullivan bluntly writes in *Rats*, his rat's-eye account of the Big Apple, "If you are in New York . . . you are within close proximity of one or more rats having sex."

Dogs were over, I thought. I'd done dogs. I was still living in the shadow of the only dog there would ever be. I still couldn't see past Agatha. It seemed easier to parallel-play, get to know a different kind of beast better. So Tito and Lolita and I would be enough. We'd be plenty.

It might be more accurate to say that I swore off people for a little bit, same as I always did when navigating the middle of the storm. Only once my heart had steadied, my tears dried, did I report back in, but never from within the tattered raw of it—though I did make one tearful call that morning to my friend Kelly. Kelly is fiercely smart, fiercely openhearted, and one of the more magical thinkers I know. She says things to me sometimes that no one else could without my going inside-out with discomfort—spiritual things, invisible energies, the touching of hands to pain. But her belief is so easy and smooth, it makes me feel better to stay close to her, to listen, to believe. That day I called her from my Brooklyn apartment, she said to me as naturally as if she were a first responder reminding me to breathe, "I want you to walk outside, find the nearest tree, and I don't care if anyone sees you, you put that tree to your forehead. Pull it right in."

The idea of doing as she'd instructed made me belly-laugh with nerves. But when we hung up, I got right to it. Just outside my lovely little apartment perch on the corner of Union and Smith, I closed my eyes and brought my forehead to the Breakup Tree.

But back to my swearing off men.

It didn't last long, thanks to my other friend Cyd. She would casually check in on me during the weeks after, at first to see how I was doing, then to casually announce that she'd met someone I had to meet. "No way," I said. "Nope." But over the course of a few weeks, she gently chipped away. He'd gone to the same college as we had. He was kind, smart, handsome, athletic. "Good for that guy," I said. "Not interested." That's when she brought down the hammer. "Did I mention he has a dog?" What had seemed like a beleaguered last-ditch effort had probably been part of her plan all along—I forgot to mention, Cyd's a lawyer. She must have known my affection for animals but had no idea that her mention of the word *dog* would set off something primal in me that I hadn't felt in years. "You did not," I said. "When shall I meet this dog?"

It turned out that I would meet Matt and his dog, Booker, who lived in New Haven, on a chaperoned dog walk with Cyd and her dog, JJ, at the Supply Ponds, not far from the Connecticut shore where Matt lived—also not far from Stony Creek, where I'd spent all of those formative, humming summers.

Driving down the shaded path toward the highly touted two, I remained skeptical but was excited, at least, to spend the afternoon with some dogs. As we got out of the car, there were Matt and Booker standing in the dappled yellow dream light near a big rock, waiting for us—for *me*. What a poem, those two. Matt was so handsome—a young Ed Harris, perhaps, with redder hair.

And how to describe Booker the dog? Wolf meets horse meets dinosaur meets tongue. He was so eager and long haired and majestic he might as well have been wearing a bow tie. When I first saw them, Booker was sitting, but when he saw Matt wave, Booker stood up and wiggled from the front of his rib cage to the tip of his tail, not because he knew us or what was to come, but simply because he'd pinned down the origin of his person's excitement and was therefore excited, too. *You! Here! Now!* Dogs are so remarkably *in* their bodies. They are present, in-the-moment beasts. With such a fundamental dependence on instinct, where better could they go?

As we walked, Cyd between Matt and me, JJ and Booker thrashed through the woods around us. Booker periodically returned to us with sticks of varying sizes in his mouth, each one bigger than the last. By the time we neared the parking lot and the end of our afternoon together, he was trying to drag a whole log.

Meanwhile, the non-stick-driven creatures chatted about nearly everything. As I talked, Matt listened with a whole history of listening in him. I interacted with Booker the way I imagine one might with the child of a love interest. I felt how important it was that Booker like me (what I didn't yet know was that Booker liked everyone)—which Matt declared he did when we stopped at a certain woodsy vista and Booker leaned his whole body up against me. "He's a leaner," Matt said. "And it only means one thing: I'm afraid you're part of the pack now."

The next day, Cyd called to tell me that Matt wanted my email address and ask if it would be okay to give it to him. Though I'd already composed a couple of letters to him in my head, I waited. Two days after we'd met, it arrived. I saw his name in my inbox and turned red with the dog-shaped glimpse at the rest of my life, my kneecaps burning like adolescence.

He wrote, "Booker and I are avid explorers of woods, marshes, and varied bodies of water (he more than I), and would love for you to join us again. I'll offer conversation. Booker's generosity includes wet leans."

I wrote, "I'd love to see you and that gorgeous wolf-horse dog of yours again. (The wet lean—doesn't that sound like something Tony Soprano would do?—was one of my favorite moments.)"

Cyd was all smiles. She knew. We knew. The trees knew. I swore off swearing off men, and Matt and I would spend nearly every weekend together. Those weekends were passionate and cinematic, our bodies at the mercy of train rides and car trips and animals and each other. We took turns commuting, our growing love ricocheting back and forth from Connecticut to New York with the zipping power of Williams sisters tennis. Even apart, we didn't feel separate. I remember beginning a shift at my job as a word processor at Skadden Arps law firm in Times Square, knowing he would later be arriving across town on a train at Grand Central, my full-body excitement sustained for seven straight hours. At the end of my ten-second elevator ride down, there he would be, his calm, beguiling face lit with every light in the city.

Once, Matt drove in and brought along Booker for a city sleepover. It was so thrilling to have a dog in my apartment, it was as if he were an actual wolf lying there. I don't think it was the best night of sleep a wolf ever had. Between the dogged sounds of the city and the giant-eyed cats eyeing him from only the highest surfaces, I don't think he slept a wink.

As I watched him trot the long Brooklyn avenues the next morning, I wondered if his urban, Midwestern heart was coming back to him. Booker had come into Matt's life six years before I met them, when Matt and his girlfriend at the time, Gail, were living in Chicago. There in the middle of a chaotic city pound, they found a filthy little lion-pawed puppy and somehow glimpsed his lion-sized heart. That relationship had ended a couple of years later when Matt headed east to New Haven for a job, Booker in the passenger seat of the U-Haul that held all of their furniture. If I know either of them, I know that Matt rolled down the window for Booker and let the fresh air thwack his tongue.

About six months after that city sleepover, Tito, Lolita, and I packed up our things and moved into Matt and Booker's house in Branford. I don't remember the moment we decided this. It was as if this were just another scheduled stop along the ride. Once I'd gotten on at the beginning, there was no questioning each stop, only learning how.

Merging furniture is one thing, beasts another, and this was a job I took seriously. The animals had all met before the move, as I'd been bringing the cats out for weekends and they'd all spent that night in Brooklyn staring at each other. Booker had already exercised and promptly dropped his instinct to chase after enduring a few hisses and airborne claws. He could have gulped the cats down for breakfast had he wanted, but he opted for self-preservation and let them run the ship. Pretty soon, whenever the cats passed by him, Booker would avert his eyes, turn his whole head, as if to say, *Jesus Christ, what the fuck is that fucking thing going to do now?* He truly was the gentlest giant. And the cats truly were a little fucking batshit sometimes.

Since I was working from home, I had lots of time to get to know Booker by myself—walking him, feeding him, taking him to his vet visits. Though I knew dogs and had grown up with them, I'd never had my *own* dog. I was technically still a kid when Agatha died. I'd never before been the adult of a dog, the mom of a dog, and truthfully, I was a little nervous. At a dog park for the first time in my life, I took a big breath before unhooking his leash with the tender trepidation of a mother hugging her child one last time before the first morning of kindergarten. With pride akin to that of watching your child make new friends, I watched Booker boldly mingle among the other butts and noses. His favorite was a collie named Dusty, whose people, Beth and her five-year-old daughter, Kira, were my favorites, too.

Booker was so front heavy and barrel-chested he seemed built to wear both a Speedo and a cape. And the ballet he choreographed with a tennis ball was pure Baryshnikov. He could fit two in his mouth, effectively safe-keeping one the whole time he ran back and forth retrieving the other. I often found him rolling around on his back on the grass, only to realize when he got up that he'd been rolling on his ball the way I now self-massage before working out. It felt so different from my devotion to Agatha. But why? *I* was certainly different, the adult now as opposed to the kid. But there was also the difference of presence and pace—my slow, steady understanding of what a dog is. I was paying attention to him, not just losing myself in him. Along with Brownie and Little Miss Tiny and my Little Me—that ever-booming voice of authority occupying my kid head—Agatha had been my rudder, my chaperone through the thick, bewildering jungle of childhood. Booker felt more like an equal. He leaned into me as hard as I leaned into him. A dog isn't an answer, but something bewitched and infinite and *other* that so willingly holds you while you wonder, while you look.

One thing Matt said Booker loved to do was run off-leash at the marsh. Around the corner from the house was a breathtaking inlet dotted with osprey nests and cut down the middle by a mile-long zipper of trolley tracks, at the end of which was the Shore Line Trolley Museum, home to nearly one hundred vintage trolley cars and what seemed like just as many volunteer conductors, otherwise known as train fanatics. When out walking the tracks, you never knew when one might slowly roll into view and require you to step aside as some relic from the past rattled by. Having grown up in the leashed world of the city, I held my breath the first time I let him go. Would he really come back? He came back, over and over. Then one day, there was a jolt as he ran, the way you can see in an instant when midtrack a racehorse goes lame. One of his back legs jerked up and he had trouble bringing it back down. He slowed, then stopped completely, looking at me with his leg in the air as if he knew the situation required something human, like hospitals and opposable thumbs.

In the examination room the next day, there was a young male vet tech with us. He didn't say anything for a few minutes as he got his papers together, then he turned to Booker and said, "Mommy's wearing her rain boots today, huh?" He proceeded to ask Booker all of the questions only I could, in human words, answer. But that's what we did. That's how we took care of business. *Candid Camera* did come to mind, but only fleetingly. He was so earnest. He asked Booker, "So how long has your leg been bothering you?" And I answered, "He injured it yesterday on a walk." In retrospect, I wish I'd been audacious and spontaneous enough to answer in Booker's voice, though there didn't seem to be an ounce of comedy or irony in this man's decision to address Booker instead of me. It might have offended him, made him feel mocked. In the face of the dog, he was just all in. And who am I to say this isn't the best way to do it, to assess an animal in pain? Or to address an animal at any time? Directly. I talk to my animals like this all the time and they often seem to understand me. Or does it seem so because I need it to be so?

In her essay in "The Lives of Animals," Barbara Smuts goes into great depth about her remarkably interactive relationship with her dog, Safi, communicating with her as an intelligent being, discussing "all important matters with her, in English, re-peating phrases and sentences over and over in particular cir-cumstances to facilitate her ability to learn [Smuts's] language." She calls dogs "nonhuman persons" in that they are not objects but social subjects "whose idiosyncratic, subjective experience of us plays the same role in their relations with us that our sub-jective experience of them plays in our relations with them." I don't know if that vet tech was familiar with Barbara Smuts or not, but I decided to believe he had tapped into something significant. We humans were taking care of my nonhuman person the best way we knew how.

With the diagnosis of a torn ACL, Booker had surgery not long after. He came home with his whole leg shaved and a long zippered line of stiches. He was an uncommonly good patient, calmly enduring the dreaded cone at least four times while I knew him. Twice, he scratched his eyeball and had to undergo a procedure that entailed an animal eye specialist (incidentally, he was very easy on the eyes), who pricked the surface of Booker's eyeball with a tiny needle around forty times. I heard every one of them. The doctor said he'd never seen a dog so uncommonly trusting, just looking him in the eye for the duration of the procedure. (My brother-in-law Michael had a similar superpower of staring down his doctor—and the pain—when getting stitches as a kid, which he reportedly did a record number of times.)

That first year living with Matt and Booker, I got my dog rhythm back—but it was a decidedly new rhythm. It was the rhythm of caretaking and decision making, not just luxuriating in the comforting company of the dog, though I still did plenty of that. Unlike with most actual stepchildren, it took a single day together for me to belong to him and him to belong to me. I was his mama. He was my baby-dog-nonhuman-person-wolf. We were, every one of us in that house, in love.

Surgery of Modern Wolfdog
(for Matt and Booker, 2006)
The pink tongue of the wolfdog
Slack with surgery.
Paws bloated with dreams and anesthesia.
Tranquil and shorn.
The owner,
Holding his breath with his eyes closed—
As if in mid-kiss—
Gripping his grandmother's rosary beads
At the end of the wrong zip code.
They are out hiking the trails together,
Man and Wolfdog.
On opposite sides of the OR wall
This mutual dream makes them tremble.

In October 2007, Whitten got married. He married Mimi, his college girlfriend, who was also a friend and squash teammate of mine. (I sometimes forget Whitten and I went to college together. We were friends, of course, always friends, but friends at a distance during those years, as if giving our childhoods and adulthoods a little respectful space to shake out.) I spent the weekend in North Carolina celebrating with all kinds of old friends. Harriet flew out from Los Angeles and the original threesome was back together. It was fun and exhausting and I came home bleary-eyed and terribly hungover.

From the couch, my legs up on his lap, I told Matt all about it as he kept handing me water. He patiently listened as I told him all kinds of inside jokes and stories about people he didn't grow up with, which made me laugh much harder than him.

"I told the Chloe-showed-me-her-vagina story at the rehearsal dinner," I said.

"Wow," he said. "You got a room full of people to picture your vagina."

"What!?" I yelled. "No I didn't! *That's* what I did!? *Really??* Nooooo."

In case anyone's curious what it's like to spend your life with a psychoanalyst, this isn't the worst glimpse.

The next afternoon, when he got home from work earlier than usual, he suggested we go on a walk at the marsh with Booker. It was a beautiful day for the excursion we so often made together.

When we reached the spot at the curve where we usually turned around, Matt suggested we go a little farther, taking us up to the lookout from which we were eye level with the ospreys braiding the air over Long Island Sound. I took in the whole panorama from neighborhood to marsh to sound, while nervously corralling Booker back from the edge of the cliff. When I turned around, my hand tightly wrapped around Booker's collar, I saw the shirt Matt had tied around his waist, floating in the air in front of him, then landing on the ground. Matt lowered to one knee on top of it. I wish I could remember his exact words, but I don't remember any of them except the general sentiment of wanting to spend the rest of his life with me and something about not having a ring because he wanted my uncle Stewart, a jeweler, to make it so we could all design it together. I dropped to my knees, too, and, speaking both to him and to the farthest-out spot in the sky that would hear me, said: *Yes!* We kissed and held each other and Booker circled us like a big hairy grouper, beating his long feather-duster tail gently on our arms and cheeks and backs like the wildest blessing.

Smell is said to be the sense most strongly connected to memory—in humans, anyway. Though it must be the case for dogs, too. The percentage of a dog's brain that's relegated to smell analysis is said to be forty times more powerful than ours, so it seems fair to say that their memories are made up of meat treats, animal scat, and body odor. You hear about dogs recognizing their owners after being lost for years, and given how much a human can physically change, that recognition must depend on the dog's nose. Otter, for one, seems to hate when I kiss him just after I've applied lotion or peppermint lip balm. He always turns his face, though maybe it's less hate than bewilderment as to where *my* smell has gone. Perhaps it makes it harder to recognize me. Though as with us, it doesn't seem to be smell and smell alone that summons things. My grandmother adopted a dog named Elle (short for Miss Elegance) who cowered at the sight of shoes, so there must have been a bad shoe memory there. Most people who've adopted dogs—dogs that come with a history beyond the two months of mother's milk and littermates—come to learn that a particular animal's triggers, good or bad, will follow it forever, life after life, unless deliberately trained out of it. If you can call the conditioning process of training a kind of memory, then the sound of a clicker or your voice saying *Yes* every time the desired behavior is performed seems to deserve some credit in the act of burrowing in. Whatever the case, humans and dogs olfactorily overlap here. We are both creatures at the mercy of the memories we smell.

When I smell cigars I will always be sitting in the swivel chairs on Higgins Lake in Michigan next to my grandfather Seaweed, his round face glowing as we take in our zillionth sunset there. When I smell rain I will always be soaked in it, desperately searching for my favorite Scottie friend; when I smell hay, I will always be at camp picking clean Chief's hooves, leaning into his warm, speckled belly, click-clacking my tongue at him to get that heavy hoof up. But, for me, music does just the same.

When I hear Bruce Springsteen's *Born in the USA*, I will always be driving to Michigan with my parents, all of us singing every word together, until the spool of the tape got so tired it simply jumped out of the cassette player, leaving us to ourselves and each other and the windows down and the friendship bracelets and Agatha's head on my knee. When I hear Bob Seger's

"We've Got Tonight," I will always be in a pharmacy in the West Village the week after Agatha died, crying in front of the wall of anti-inflammatories at the words: "I know your plans they don't include me. . . ." When I hear "The Aspidistra Flies" by Stars, I will always be dancing with Matt in his house before I moved in, singing along to "All the umbrellas in London / Couldn't hide my love for you . . .," not knowing that seven months later I would live in that house, too. And when I hear Sufjan Stevens's album *Carrie & Lowell*, I will always be back in 2015, navigating the long, rickety months before Booker died.

When I play that album now, four years after Booker's death, I wonder if music carries with it memories for dogs, too. I wonder what a dog's memory *is*. Does the album also bring Safari back to those heavy waiting days? If I've heard it one million times, he has, too. I wonder if he thinks, *Not this again*, or *Oh! Friend! This!*

In the opening shot of *High Fidelity*, John Cusack's pale, head-phoned Rob Gordon asks the camera: "What came first? The music or the misery? People worry about kids playing with guns or watching violent videos, that some sort of culture of violence will take them over. Nobody worries about kids listening to thousands, literally thousands, of songs about heartbreak, rejection, pain, misery, and loss. Did I listen to pop music because I was miserable or was I miserable because I listened to pop music?" I don't think I'd go as far as to say I was miserable because I listened to pop music, but I do wish someone had staged an intervention or two during my first thirty years. The way it has always worked for me is that in feeling miserable I turn to music, whereupon I feel even more miserable, which is, of course, the point. But it's also true that I have wished on many frozen-peas-to-the-swollen-crying-eyes occasions that someone would just come and take my music away.

In musical terms, at least, I've always been in good touch with my misery. The same way that dogs have helped me shoulder heavy burdens and my imagination has allowed for bigger explorations than I'd dare make on Earth, music has guided me from the extremes of my emotional well-being straight to the big, messy feelings I've always craved. Since being a mess in my childhood didn't feel like an option, I would fling myself toward the easiest method of bringing the mess on while still controlling it. I knew I could press "Stop" and clean it all away. Like the dogs, music could hold the parts of me no one else could.

Though something shifted not far into my relationship with Matt. By then, I'd been in therapy for a couple of years, long enough to notice that as I talked more, I felt more, and as I felt more, I didn't need the music as much. (I prayed this would never be true of dogs.) I still loved it but didn't need it to guide me toward what feeling felt like. It began accompanying my emotions, not commanding them. I no longer depended on it to comfort me or, more important, tell me how I was feeling. I *felt* how I felt. *That* was my discomfort (and my comfort) now. Along with the knowledge that Matt and I would do the work no matter what Bruce or Sufjan had to say about it. I could finally hear songs the way they were meant to be heard, as music, rather than merely as triggers for the memories I played over and over in my heart and head. Perhaps it was the difference of having such a tangible future now: Matt and his entire history of songs and dogs.

When it came to choosing music for our wedding ceremony, Matt and I had many ideas. We chose no music. My parents and I walked as a trio through my dad's ravishing garden (in

1994, my parents bought their own property in Stony Creek just up the hill from the Ellses and had spent more than two decades transforming it from a mud pit to a paradise), our feet trotting toward Matt, dad of Booker, past Agatha's grave, which only seemed fitting since in the dog version of that day, I married Booker; Agatha gave me away. We processed to the sporadic ringing of an old family farm bell rung by our nephew, Cook.

We began our married life dancing in the middle of a beloved crowd. It's not that we couldn't come up with music that felt personal—there are plenty of songs and sentiments that feel like *ours*. We opted for trees and birds and bells because of all that could be expressed without music. We wanted something we'd never heard before and we'd never hear again.

Immediately after the ceremony, as it rained like a murmuration of starlings, our friend Erin, one of Booker's best humans, said she heard him bark just as we exchanged vows. She'd understandably assumed he was on the premises—tucked safely in my parents' house somewhere while we wed. Even though the truth was we'd left him at our home, eight miles down the road, I didn't tell her. I just smiled, because, even eight miles down the road, I am certain she was right.

Safari: Dog of Motherhood

(2008-present)

Though I love telling my human story of how Matt and I met, I sometimes let myself wonder about Booker's version. Dogs are such present beasts. They never seem too caught up in the agony of what was, of what no longer is. But surely he must have known Gail, his first mom, was suddenly missing. Everything I know of her says she was fun and loving and kind. She was the one who saw that grungy pound puppy and glimpsed something magnificent, and for that, I have always been grateful. He must have sensed in the towering green ecstasy of the lowered U-Haul window that this throne of his should have been hers. He should have been in the back or between them. He must have seen that Matt was sad and that the early days of single-parenting him around the demands of a new city and job weren't easy. But they found the park. They met Dale the human and his spaniel, Ruby. They met other humans, Erin and Lauren and Mark, the latter two of whom would become Booker's Monday–Friday parents, driving him out to their suburban house and yard in Guilford, where he could nest with Lauren and her brand-new baby, Kyla. He must have had opinions about the women Matt dated, but maybe I say that because I want to imagine that when I came along, he also loved me best; he loved me completely. He finally saw not only a friend and mother in me but Matt's Big Love, the kind of love that sits and stays, waits with the big, warm towel while you swim.

Fresh off the teetering heels of single life in Brooklyn, I was elated to be all of these things to Matt and Booker. The novelty of a *home—our* home—cast such a bewitching spell. I'd found a man and dog looking for love, and they'd found a love looking for a man and dog. Even now, as I look around me more than a decade later, it is not lost on me that the cup of fresh pens on my desk and the wall-to-wall carpet beneath my feet are because of Booker. The entire shape of my adult life was thanks to the wet lean of this one colossal dog. Matt is undoubtedly why I stayed, but Booker is the only reason I showed up in the first place. Which is why when he had his ACL surgeries, then another to remove a cancerous lump on his head, the earth under my heart began to shake.

It's been like this for as long as I can remember: the more madly I love you, the more often I picture losing you. I've probably even written a few lines of your eulogy in my head. Though he was in great general health, Booker was eight, now technically a senior, so as we followed him through the woods and hunkered down with him on the living room floor, forehead-to-forehead, our eyes inches out from his, losing him was already a looming sorrow. At the same time, it felt impossible that there would come a day when this majestic beast wouldn't breathe anymore. My eyes foggy, it began to occur to me that the only solution to bearing the inevitable disappearance of *such* an incredible dog was to get another dog as soon as possible so that all of his greatness had a tangible place to go—another fuzzy body to live on in. So I commenced the most unfaithful period of my marriage, a few winter weeks spent secretly bingeing on my own version of late-night porn, otherwise known as Petfinder. During this dander bender, I found myself regularly and unconvincingly slamming the computer shut on eight saved puppy profiles whenever Matt walked into the room, the screen filled with descriptions like: *Sweet and playful, cat-friendly shepherd mix with huge paws; Social and active Flat-coat retriever baby who loves belly scratches and everyone he's ever met; Timid but trying chocolate lab mix with a white heart on her forehead.* I mean, c'mon!

"Whatcha up to?" Matt would say.

"Oh, research," I'd tell him.

It wasn't until I settled on a husky/collie litter from Georgia, which would be available for a meeting in a neighboring town on an upcoming weekend, that I came clean.

It wasn't easy. I don't mean just because Matt didn't share the same burning dog-living-on-in-another-dog theory, I mean because this was the exact kind of decision and requisite conversation that most highlighted our different desires. I wanted to bring more beasts into our life; he wanted us to feel more comfortably human. Though it had been more than a decade since Agatha had died, and though Matt had never met her, he knew my stubborn old ways of being the dog well. I'd undoubtedly done a lot of growing in that decade, but the reintroduction of dogs in my life, the magical emergence of Booker, was enough permission for me to sometimes want to be him, to turn away from my adult responsibilities and my marriage and go dog. And it didn't occur to me at the time that Matt might not have heard this idea of another dog the way I meant it—as an honor, a tribute, a desperate measure at a love-filled time. He might have just heard in it the word *replacement*. And though his childhood was sprinkled with dogs, Booker was the only dog Matt had ever become. And though I know they were very happy to find me, my sudden and constant presence (with cats!) surely cut through a bit of their man's-best-friend-I'll-be-on-my-couch-you-be-on-yours spell. The moment they met me could in fact be seen as the beginning of Matt's losing him. And now, in Booker's final act, I was asking Matt to love and become another dog the way he longed for us to become each other. I don't know if he ever thought about other dogs, envisioned them the way I did in our future. But I know he envisioned *us*.

We were lying on the beach under a tropical, turtle sun on our honeymoon in St. John and he'd asked, "You're thinking about the dogs right now, aren't you?"

"Yes," I told him.

He was my husband now; I'd promised the truth.

We laughed, but I knew there was pain in this. The good news was, the person my husband was most likely to find me spooning other than him was a dog. The bad news was, it was *a dog*. As much as I'd relied on dogs to take in my truths over the years, I hadn't chosen a life with just dogs. I'd chosen human love, and marriage—to a *psychoanalyst*, of all improbable beasts. I'd agreed to children—*two*, when I only knew the experience of being *one*. I'd chosen a house full of movement and emotion when I didn't know how to make sense of conflict. I chose messy and loud when I've never been either. Not on the outside, anyway.

If it's a therapist's job to help us figure out why we are the way we are, it's ours alone to want to see it—but there's always a reason. A reason some of us never feel adequate. A reason some of us drink. A reason some of us would prefer to smash our faces into a dog than wrestle with a fellow human being. My reason for needing dogs (and animals in general) has always seemed lazily linked to wanting sweet and cute. In fact, it's much deeper. I've needed dogs because their unapologetic, effortless need has given me permission to need, too.

Matt, on the other hand, doesn't just like to talk—not about the weather, but us—he needs to, as much as I up to this point had needed to smash my face in a dog. It's what I'd learned to do so often in the place of emotional truth. So I'm not going to pretend that how we got Safari was by some bighearted joint joy. But it was by an act of love that Matt agreed to accompany me late one night to pick out our pup from the four remaining when our adoption application had been approved.

Safari's was an unwanted backyard litter that didn't have a lot of human contact during their first few months of life, though they appeared to be in beautiful condition, their coats shiny and plush, and so were fairly face-shy. They were all submissive and sweet. They seemed cared for, if not maybe wanted or loved. They clearly *wanted* to be loved but didn't know how to let themselves be loved. The feeling was familiar.

Though the pup that had gotten my attention online had already been adopted, it didn't take long for us to agree on Matsi, the fuzzy golden boy who, to us, was the most beautiful but also the shyest of the bunch. This latter detail worried Matt a little, which I understood, because you never know how that will translate in a home that will hopefully also house kids one day. But I didn't share this worry. While Booker was the ambassador of dogs, this anxious little guy already felt like the dog version of me. The way he curled into my lap on our first drive home with him felt like both love *and* disappearance, like he wanted whatever those arms around him meant, but he also seemed terrified at the directness of physical touch. I felt the same way about human love all the time.

For his first few nights, we kept him in the bathroom off our bedroom. I gave him my childhood stuffed animal donkey, Abraham—there's no law against keeping stuffed animals into your thirties, you know—and pretty soon the pair were sleeping downstairs in the living room with Booker. One of my favorite sights of all time was watching baby Safari drag Abraham, who was easily three times bigger than him, around the room, climb on top of him, and go to sleep. Eventually, because our fluffball was a *real* dog, not a fantasy one, he ate Abraham's eyes and nose, and when he discovered all the fun stuffing inside, we had to let poor Abraham go. RIP to the best stuffed donkey for getting us both through those scared early nights of child- and puppyhood.

It took a week to settle on it, but we named him Safari. One afternoon, while holding him belly-up on my lap, I remarked that he looked like a coyote, wolf, fox, lion, and seal all stuffed into one. "Like a safari," Matt said. "Safari!" we both shouted, knowing we'd chosen the right pup. "'It's love,' they say," writes William Stafford in his poem "Choosing a Dog." "You touch / the right one and a whole half of the universe / wakes up, a new half."

I'll never forget setting him down in the yard that first night and letting Booker out to meet him. Safari's whole body came instantly alive, as if his fluffy, wiggling self was shouting, "My people! My people!" Or, rather, "My wolf! My wolf!" From that moment on, he hardly left Booker's side. While I can't say this development was immediately Booker's bliss (Booker would have bonded with a Tasmanian devil), within a month or two their limb-tangled naps and fur-crossed car trips clearly contained mutual affection. I can see now why some might say I missed an opportunity with him. Instead of fully treating his anxiety, tirelessly training him until he snapped out of it, I treated it, but met him and loved him from deep within it, too. I solidified it. I normalized it. I understood it, and probably because I still had so much work to do on my own, I treated it not as something to change completely but as part of what comes with loving him, perhaps because it is undoubtedly part of what comes with loving me, too. We could keep each other company in it. While I have worked hard to make him feel more comfortable, more loved and secure, I could have done more to deeply desensitize some of his fears—like greeting new people and those trolleys that suddenly rumbled through the marsh. He'd hear them coming before I did and immediately pull toward home. Once, when I'd let him off-leash with Booker, his trolley panic overtook him and, before I could catch him, he ran all the way home by himself, navigating our coastal roads by eyesight as my heart completely lost balance. He was terrified, but he knew where to go. His safe place. When I arrived there, too, completely out of breath from having sprinted, there he was sitting by our gate, waiting. *Home.*

I did take Safari to puppy training classes to try to help him gain confidence, but he was so nervous amid the chaotic scene, and so terrified of the loud air conditioner in the corner that he wouldn't walk past, that the trainer graduated us without going through the final test. That last day, she'd gotten so frustrated at his refusal to go near the air conditioner that she took him from me and worked with him herself, pulling him closer and closer while trying to feed him treats he was too scared to eat. I'm not sure she didn't do more damage to him that day. She reminded me of an exasperated parent telling their terrified child that there's nothing to be afraid of. I took our diploma and left. He knew what he needed to know. He knew who his people were. He knew where he was safe and loved. And in my world that put him in a better place than most humans.

Can dogs and humans exist without love? Yes. But not thrive. That seems to be the pivotal trait domestication bred. Wild animals don't need love to thrive—not in the human definition anyway. They need roles to fulfill, systems to carry out, orders to follow. But an animal living among humans understands that love, or the lack thereof, has consequences and learns to live within its sturdy sway.

What helped Safari most, of course, was also the reason the rescue we adopted him from was so thrilled with our application—we had an elder dog. Safari had in his arsenal the greatest buoy-buddy, the most loyal lifeline of all: Booker. For the first seven years of his life, anyway, it's impossible to talk about Safari without talking about the great, big beast in whom Safari found his inner dog. He followed Booker everywhere. He learned from Booker that it was fine to be off-leash in the woods, but you never want to get too far, you never want to get so dog about it that you go completely wolf and lose your humans for good. He learned from Booker that getting in the car almost always meant good things—walks in the woods or by the water, getting to go with the family on vacation rather than being left at home. He learned his own limitations from Booker, too. The one place Safari wouldn't follow Booker was into the water, and Booker couldn't pass a body of water without fully jumping in. So Safari learned to walk in up to his dewclaws and dutifully pace the shore while his comrade went for a dip. He learned to trust that it was temporary, that Booker would always return to share with Safari his solo adventure by exultantly shaking it all over him. But that wasn't enough. Safari had to sniff him tongue to tail. It was like watching the dog version of a military spouse welcoming his or her soldier back from a war zone. And concerning the vexing business of cats, Safari certainly took cues from Booker, too, but he took his most memorable feline direction directly from Lolita. I don't know what exactly transpired, but I came downstairs one morning to find Lolita up on the kitchen counter and Safari in the corner, a perfect line of blood slashed across the top of his nose. I don't think he ever even looked at her again, though from that day on, whenever they were in the room together, Safari would let out the softest little whimper, a whimper I came to understand as the sound of a peaceable kingdom.

Like the presence of any young life, Safari's youth brought out more of Booker's, and in one of the most vivid, moving examples of love and trust I've ever seen, Booker gradually coaxed Safari out of his shell. *He*, not *we*, taught Safari to trust his humans, to love his humans—and, in turn, allow himself to be loved.

While I hope there are plenty of dogs still to come, if everyone has that One Dog, that Heart Dog, that dog that's meant to be, mine is unequivocally Safari, or Safi, as we sometimes call him. Yes, I feed him and care for him; he knows he needs me. And though I would like to think that it's laser-beam love that draws him to me during thunderstorms and when we're navigating a house that's not ours, a place he's never before been, science tells me it's something closer to instinct. But add a little heart to that science and I feel like his twin *and* his mother. When he flees, he flees to me. I am his One Person, his Heart Girl, the human that was meant to be.

I think of Safari as a dog who sometimes (like me) pretends to be a dog but is really (like me) quite human. He often seems to me like he's faking the whole being-a-dog business. While walking him recently, I stopped, so he did, too. "Wanna sniff?" I asked. I very much believe in not rushing dogs on walks, letting them sniff to their heart's content, lighting up those nose and brain receptors like crossword puzzles do for the elderly. He understands what this means and so veers off the path a little to sniff some grass, but it's like he's just playing the part, not even looking at it or taking in the nose-boggling information the grass is giving him. He keeps his nose there for what seems like the dog-appropriate amount of time, then looks at me as unmoved as a human who'd just sniffed grass. *Was that enough?* his eyes go. *Am I dog enough for you now?* When we walk on the local public trails, he never takes his eyes off the creepy psychos (totally normal people) around us, but neither do I. They're all creepy psychos. He once came out of the woods behind our house with a baby bunny in his mouth. Not even this was convincing. I told him to drop it and he did with such haste it was as if he was filled with relief, like he'd been thinking, *Good God, who do I think I am? For Christ's sake, someone take this dear babe off my fangs!* Occasionally he looks at his paws with disgust, as if he's embarrassed they're not hands. I wouldn't be the least bit surprised if I unzipped his fur only to find a little human. Sometimes when I'm writing he walks over and hooks one of his paws over my arm. When I look at him and say, "Hey, buddy. What's happening? What's the scoop?" he looks at me with such enormous, vibrating eyes that I still believe he'll start talking in full sentences one day.

And in which language? I feel pretty certain Safari is Welsh the same way I'm betting that Booker was French Canadian. Booker, likely the genial, strapping captain of a downhill ski team, and Safari, an earnest, self-effacing, barely audible tour guide in Cardiff. Both swear like trucks.

I've read their dating profiles, too.

Booker: "Bighearted, totally undiscerning wolfdog looking for more love to lean on. I don't care who. Peed in your pants? I bet your crotch smells awesome. Oh, and I've got a *huge* tongue. Just sayin'. DM me, *mes amis*."

Safari: "Gorgeous (my mom's word, not mine) husky/collie mix looking for mellow, risk-free adventures—no, let's not say 'adventures,' let's say 'running fun circles in the safety of our own yards.' I enjoy tennis balls, but only ones that the lawn mower has viciously split in two, preferably not all the way through, but *almost* all the way so that they fetchingly flap. I can't promise you a rose garden, but I will softly smudge the back of your knees with the damp velvet of my nose as you carry my food bowl to its stand. Anyone? If not, no big whoop."

On February 18, 2009, I took a pregnancy test that revealed two strong pink lines—a dizzying, sure sign that our human family was now growing. I left it on the bathroom sink for Matt to discover and spent the afternoon walking around like I was holding the world's biggest secret. We'd met smack in the middle of our fertile years, after we'd spent almost two decades in trial-and-error with members of the opposite sex, so when we knew, the way you know when choosing a dog, our trajectory took on the kind of momentum NASA would appreciate. Within a couple of years, I'd moved from Brooklyn, we'd gotten married, and now I was pregnant. I'd been in other relationships for longer still trying to determine, *How is this going?* And here we were, flying together, adding more flesh to our house that fur built.

At eighteen weeks, we learned we were having a boy. That was the precise moment I realized how easily, almost lazily, I had already decided we were having a girl. Not by any sorcery tricks or cosmic signs; merely because that is what *I* was, that was what I *knew: girl.* What on Earth was I supposed to do with a *boy?* And *that* was the precise moment I began to laugh at how delightfully unexpected this was, how absurd even, like I had truly not once considered that statistically this outcome had been just as likely from the beginning. A boy! Even crazier: he was due on Halloween.

We didn't tell anyone, but we already knew his name: Jackson. He would be named for Jackson, Ohio, where Matt's mother Gwyneth's family had put down their Welsh roots and up grew pig iron.

Halloween 2009. Jackson's due date. In about an hour, our friends Lin and Eileen were coming over with homemade lamb burgers. Since I don't eat lamb, they were kindly bringing alternatives—but at forty weeks pregnant, I wasn't feeling hungry for much.

My parents dropped by to say hi, and just before they did, I felt a brief, slight cramp and thought, *If I have this baby tonight then that was my first contraction*. My mom still talks about the stricken look on my face that I was trying to hide when I opened the door. Sure enough, an hour later, I had another. When Lin and Eileen arrived, we told them, but there was no reason to cancel dinner. From everything we'd learned, this was the longest stretch—waiting for that magic number: ten centimeters—which could take hours, and the last thing you wanted to do, we were told, was arrive at the hospital too early and get sent home. So we carried on under the assumption that my labor would go that way. But it wasn't long before the intensity of the contractions was enough that I had to start excusing myself from the table to endure each one alone upstairs. There, I could focus on my breathing and get some space for the pain. As each contraction arrived faster and significantly stronger than the last, the doorbell never stopped ringing as trick-or-treaters came and went. I could hear Matt saying over and over, "Oh *wow*, look at *you*! Great costume! Happy Halloween!" This is when I stopped coming down. I stayed in our bedroom on my hands and knees, huffing through each wave as Booker and Safari paced and whimpered around me. I was already feeling like the situation had gotten away from me and was about to call out for Matt when he walked in. He called the doctor, who was out trick-or-treating with his kids. They talked things through a bit, but when the doctor heard that my first contraction was only a couple of hours ago, he said it was most likely still too early to come to the hospital. I shook my head and Matt told him I was in a lot of pain and out of breath and we both felt like it was time. He asked Matt to put me on the phone. I could barely form a sentence—the exact sign, it turns out, he was looking for—so he told Matt he would meet us at the hospital as soon as possible.

Lin and Eileen were already quietly and tenderly cleaning up dinner as we headed out the door with our hospital bag—though I swear not without my husband answering the door one more time with that great, big bowl of candy. It occurred to me on the hustled walk to the car that I hadn't said goodbye to the dogs, and that they must have been worried seeing me so distraught and now disappearing into the dark world outside the window. Though what is a goodbye to a dog? I've always heard you're not supposed to make a big deal about leaving a dog because they don't understand and heavy interaction just before disappearing can make the separation more anxiety filled. So I've always said, "Be right back," and walked out the door. Dogs are organized around human routines. It's amazing to me how quickly they learn them and how their awareness of them makes me suddenly aware of them, too. Keys, a coat zipper, the pulling on of boots—all signs to them I'm about to walk out the door. *With or without me?* they always want to know, which is most vividly answered by the other detail they are looking for: *Leash or no leash?* Accordingly, they either prance about with excitement or, in Safari's case, slink off into the living room like Eeyore. This time seemed extreme though, unusual. Surely a dog knows *distress.* A study on dog empathy out of Johns Hopkins suggests dogs who saw their owners crying behind a glass door, as opposed to just humming, tried to get to their owners significantly faster than the dogs of the humming owners. I was not only leaving, I was leaving making noises I'd never made before. But I was in way too much pain to get much farther in this thought before we were ripping down the shoreline road and I was asking my husband to drive faster for the first time ever.

A security guard signaled a nurse, who appeared with a wheelchair at the hospital entrance when they saw that I could hardly stand. There was no time for paperwork. The doctor and nurses were already delighting at the prospect of a Halloween baby—a little goblin, perhaps! But midnight passed. Close to three hours after I'd begun pushing, I was still pushing, and though I'd made some progress, this baby wasn't coming out. I was so exhausted and in *so* much pain, pain so strong that every time it hit I'd leave my body and flash out somewhere—to the stars, to the sea, to the synthetic core of the fluorescent lighting. There were no colors. Only the pain followed.

The doctor came back into the room just before one in the morning to express concern. Four hours was too long, the baby's heart rate had dropped, and if I didn't get him out in the next several pushes, they were going to have to perform a C-section, news that was particularly crushing after four hours of pushing. I was done. Done with the whole thing. There was no way I could endure an epidural and surgery now. He asked if I wanted him to try the vacuum suction first—the top of our son's head was just visible. I looked at my husband and said, "Whatever anyone thinks." So the doctor went ahead and on the second suctioned push, at 1:04 a.m. on November 1, out came Jackson Britton Shaw, the dearest, pinkest, blotchiest, fuzziest wriggling baby thing I'd ever seen in my whole life. My husband cut his umbilical cord and there he was, snuggled in like a wild thing against my chest.

The next day, at my request, my husband took a blanket Jackson had been wrapped in home and dropped it on the living room floor so that Tito and Lolita and Booker and Safari could smell him, meet him, know him on their own terms, before they would get to see the real-life boy we'd made.

The truth is I'd been preparing them for this day for months. There was no room for them not to accept him because I wasn't under any circumstances giving any of them up, so the only alternative would be to build another house for them to live in next to ours, the funding for which was going to be a hard thing to get my husband behind. So I was motivated. Periodically, I'd place my computer in the middle of the living room rug and play a recording of a baby crying I'd found online (which frankly wasn't bad practice for my nerves either). Sure enough, the first time I played it, the cats stalked the house like slow-motion panthers, like Armageddon had officially arrived. But by the ninth or tenth, they barely turned their heads. Safari's eyes had gone gradually from *The sky is falling!* to *This weird thing again?* Booker, the only one who'd been around babies before, wasn't bothered in the least. I'd also set up our stroller months ahead and rolled it to the middle of the living room so the animals could approach it, sniff it at their leisure. Then I periodically rolled it around them. This initially sent Safari into orbit—or rather, up the stairs—but he, too, gradually adjusted. I stopped the stroller routine just short of taking them for a walk with it, sparing the neighbors the sight of a woman with two dogs pushing an empty stroller, though one website devoted to pet life went even farther, suggesting I put a doll in it, which wouldn't have looked deranged at all.

Whatever I did, it worked. Jackson and the beasts were a pack of their own now. Was he one of them or us? I didn't yet know. I was too enamored with my baby boy and too astonished by

Safari. This was the dog whose heart rate blew up at the sound of a plastic bag. The dog who hid behind me from wind. That same dog turned into the most unexpected baby whisperer there ever was. Somewhere amid the comfort of the loving home we'd given him and the chaos of a milk-thirsty baby, he'd become another warm, calm, watchful dog a family could grow around. It was as if bringing this bundle of indeterminate disorder closer to him somehow *contained* the dread of life and tucked it into this swell-smelling swaddle. The baby was messy and unpredictable, but that mess and disorder was touchable, reachable, and so, understood. To a degree at least, Jackson deactivated Safari's Fear of Everything and broke it up into workable bits. He seemed to finally understand that there were things he didn't love and things he did love, and finally, he knew the difference. He trusted, and because he trusted, he could choose. He could control. Since then, Safari has grown into his own version of dog ambassador, having won over the hearts of several local dog-phobic kids. It's something about his teddy-bear face and his great poof of fluff that makes him the one kids want to hug the most. And when they do, it's the way his big old-man eyes, his soft, shiny nose, get up so close and gently burrow in. It's as if, in him, they, too, see a version of themselves.

For the first six months of Jackson's life, we all did nothing but stare at him, breathe in all the breath he breathed out. I loved life with a newborn more than I could ever have known was possible. I hunkered down for the winter with my baby and my animals and my husband, busily coming and going from his private practice, now the sole financial support of the household.

Jackson's first couple of years rolled along a lot like that—cozy, beastly, sheltered—in the little house by the marsh and shore. But that house that Matt had bought long before he knew all the many lives that would live there started to feel too small. We'd begun talking about trying for another baby, though we were, so far, taking turns being the advocate for that thought. Even so, as Jackson grew, so did his need for more space. We found and fell in love with a house several towns inland where, upon our first visit, I felt I could live in the yard alone. It didn't just feel like a home, it felt like *our* home. What I didn't notice until we moved in that January of 2011, me now ten weeks pregnant with a second baby, was that the weathervane on top of the garage was a dog.

While unpacking I was going through some paperwork, preparing to file it, when I came across the records from Jackson's birth. I'd never seen them before, so I took a moment to nostalgically read through them. At the end, in a section simply titled "Doctor's Notes," the doctor had written just two words: *Inefficient pusher.* I imagine this must be a technical term doctors use to explain why a birth took longer than everyone thought it would—at least I hope it is—but for years these words would sting. I would tell the story to other moms and we'd all roll our eyes at the male doctor who'd written them. But as the years passed and I began facing my undeniable avoidances in other arenas of my life—being the dog at times when it was most critical that I be the human—I came to a better understanding of how the escape I made that day was in fact quite different from what the escape of being the dog is, and was. I *had* left my body, the same way I had as a young girl being groped on the street. A dissociative response seemed understandable, appropriate even, a survival tactic that rendered the assault less vivid and, perhaps, less painful. The same was true in childbirth. I wasn't *being the dog* according to the definition that I was still in my body but giving the bits of me that didn't fit in the world of humans to the dog to hold. I was gone completely, and who really knows where. No place that could contain me, anyway, no space that could hold me while I myself was too much to hold. I was overwhelmed by pain, and while I suppose somewhere in the shocked, infinitesimal crosshairs of whatever consciousness I still possessed, I'd hoped for a similar survival effect in leaving my body behind on the bed, in retrospect, this was quite counterproductive to the task at hand. More than anything else, my *body* needed me. And I was gone. It wasn't a choice but an instinct—an instinct I wish hadn't taken over that day, but one I wholly understand. It was a scorching pain, a pain so ferocious it was wordless. And the amazing thing is, my body did it anyway. Maybe, while I was floating, the dog I was trying to be had been there, after all.

The idea that this second baby had been conceived in our first house (our first *home*, the one we fell in love in) but would be born into our new one delighted me. Though a moving company called 2 Young Studs ultimately made the bulk of the move for us, the new house was only half an hour from the old, so during the weeks leading up, I drove carload after carload out, sometimes with my dad following in his own filled-to-the-brim station wagon, promising myself not to lift anything too heavy. I will never know if some small breach in this silent pact was responsible, but, a few weeks later, I found blood in my underwear

while changing out of my unpacking clothes. My mind immediately corrected its own concern by highlighting the memory
of something I'd learned during my first pregnancy when I actually spent time reading books on the topic: some spotting during
pregnancy is normal. *It's just spotting*, I told myself, and got back
to the boxes. I remember it was a Friday because there was the
weekend sitting before me and I decided it was unnecessary to
call the doctor.

My Weekend of Blood, as I know it now. By Saturday, it was
clear this was no spotting. It was blood and tissue, and, somewhere
in the middle of it all, our second baby. That was confirmed first
thing Monday morning by my doctor. I'd worn my favorite long
winter sweater. My Miscarriage Sweater, that day. As a nurse gently led me to the back door so that I didn't have to walk through
a waiting room full of pregnant women, I called my husband,
who was getting my son a Miscarriage Doughnut, and told him
I was ready to go home.

I knew how common miscarriages were, that we only think
of them as not that way because people don't tend to talk about
them. Surprisingly, the first thing I felt like doing when I got
into bed, crying, was to talk about it. I called my mom. She
hadn't known yet that I was pregnant—no one but my husband
did—so I had to deliver the happy and sad news all in one
ghostly gasp. I didn't ask, but she said she'd pack a bag and drive
to us that afternoon. *Mommy*, I could feel my body go. I'd been
in my early thirties and pregnant with Jackson when I learned
she'd had the miscarriage after me. I'd straight-out asked my parents over lunch why they chose to have only one child. After
some awkward fits and starts, my dad finally said, "We didn't."
Until then, I'd always been led to believe they'd only wanted me.

Does that still make me an only child, Dog? Can't desire alone fill an invisible sister or brother up? And is that invisible sister or brother the one who took this little snail? Who am I with or without my sibling ghost? Still me?

Safari lay on the rug at the side of my bed as I emailed my close friends and family to share the news so as not to feel so alone with it. *This happened*, as so many of my stories had gone before. But instead of speaking in the past tense, now I was saying, *This is happening. I hurt right now.*

I didn't know what to make of this change, why or how it had come about. I only thought of E. L. Doctorow saying of writing that it's like driving at night—you can only see as far as your headlights, but you can go the whole way like that. There I was, carving my way around the bends in the blacktop, unaware not only of what was next but of who, as with Safari's life trajectory, I was becoming along the way.

After a few days, I was feeling better, and sick of lying in bed devouring *Grey's Anatomy* for the first time, so I wandered out into our yard with the dogs for fresh air. It was almost February. It was cold. There was snow on the ground. I stood looking at the trees for a while, feeling surrounded by their thick hooves instead of filled up by the absence inside my body. I put my hand on the Japanese maple closest to the center of the yard and thought of what Kelly had said when I was sad in Brooklyn, swearing off men. I leaned in and pressed my forehead to the bark. I don't remember if my husband and son were home, if they could see me. I didn't care. I just knew for the moment I would press my head into the Miscarriage Tree. With my eyes closed, I saw the yard as it was in summer, my son carving paths through the forest brush and circling the lawn before we went flat to watch the bats go bonkers overhead, the dogs rolling and sniffing the edge of the woods where one day they would both be buried.

One year later and I was pregnant again—four months so. At eighteen weeks, we found out that it was a girl. That Christmas, we were still debating when to tell our little boy about the forthcoming baby girl when a gift arrived from Aunt Harriet.

"Here's to arms and legs in 2013!" her card read.

The tadpole had arrived in the mail in the middle of a blizzard, so it really was magical to slice open the transport bag and watch him wriggle with life.

"I have my own pet, Mom!" Jackson announced.

I tried not to give any indication that tadpoles didn't count as pets to me. A pet was something warm and soft you could hold in your hand, kiss on the head, maybe. A pet received your love and loved you back. A pet was a *friend*. A pet was a *dog*. And a tadpole was not a dog. Still, his words lodged in my kid heart; the first-pet milestone was not lost on me.

Caspar Frogpants—a leggy nod to Caspar Babypants, one of his favorite kid bands at the time. Jackson took this responsibility more seriously than I'd imagined he would, dutifully checking every morning on his pet, who'd been placed on a high, cat-proof shelf, asking me to carry the aquarium down to the kitchen so Caspar could "be with the family." Jackson drew pictures on sticky notes and stuck them face-in against the tank so Caspar could "have art." For better or worse, it's my fault he was this way. Not long after Caspar arrived, I announced to my husband that although we were leaving the dogs and cats behind when we traveled to New York City for Christmas, the tadpole was coming with us. Though in the end I decided the car trip would be harder on the little guy (the tadpole, not my husband) than the loneliness.

Despite my tendency toward the soft and cuddly, I, too, fell hard for our Caspar. I loved changing his tank, making it all fresh and clean for him. I loved watching Jackson compare him to the pictures of tadpoles in the books we borrowed from the library. I loved being part of the nurturing process by which he would one day grow legs. It wasn't hard for me to fall for a gloopy little fin with a head, after all. There was something simpler about this relationship than my relationship with the dogs, something more elemental. There was so much I *didn't* know: facial expressions, body language, signs of a thriving life. Since we couldn't hold him or take him out for walks, there was only so much to do with Caspar. We watched him, fed him, changed his water. And that was it. There was a little relief in the simplicity of him, like the rare math class I took amid all the arts. You're either right or you're wrong; you either know the tadpole or you don't. There is no emotion to get seduced by.

All the while, I wondered, did the dogs know he was there? I'd caught Tito watching him with his teeth one morning, as predators do. But did Safari and Booker have a clue? Did our house smell now of slime and brine? Did my love feel spread more thinly? My heart had certainly been feeling shattered.

A week earlier, I'd arrived home after dropping Jackson off at preschool in New Haven when I started hearing about a shooting at an elementary school in Newtown, not so far up the road. By the one o'clock pickup time, we'd received an email from the school acknowledging the tragedy so near to our home.

Our school director asked that, due to our children's young ages, we not discuss it with each other or our teachers during pickup. And so I found myself among a throng of desperately silent, desperately knowing adults, all holding ourselves together as we bundled up our bundles merely by not looking each other in the eyes. I spent the rest of the day in the still-magic, still-oblivious world of my chatty little boy. I didn't cry until my husband got home and I volunteered to pick up our takeout just for the time in the car alone. I listened to NPR and sobbed. At a stoplight, I looked around me—*Anyone else out there feel like this?*—and caught two others crying into the red light I think we all wished would never end, because: then what? Outside was a darkness that felt like a reminder of the downside of *not* being the dog, of being *woman, mother, human*—the ripe pain of being *too* human and the recognition that in our most elemental predilections, how haywire things can go when humans are animals, too. I was Woman, Mother, Human, Dog, *and* Tadpole now. Where did that leave me in my body? Which was the thing that held me? Who did that mean I was now?

When I found Caspar at the bottom of his aquarium early in the New Year, he was flashing me his long bright belly. Instead of popping to life as he usually did the minute I moved the tank, he made a half dozen rolls across the bottom. I started to cry—for my son, for my Caspar, for my own history of dead pets. Each time I'd lost an animal, I swore I'd never love another.

When I told Jackson we'd lost Caspar, he turned red for a moment, then promised a bit too emphatically that he was fine. *No, no, no.* I thought. *Anything but fine.*

I told him it was okay to be sad.

"I think I know why Caspar died," he said.

"Why?"

"We didn't bring him downstairs today." Then he pressed Play on his Buzz Lightyear CD player and Vampire Weekend's *Modern Vampires of the City* came on.

He looked out the window as I walked into the kitchen to clean out Caspar's tank and figure out what to do with the body. Jackson was right. We'd forgotten. It was the one day Caspar hadn't had family time, which was, for me, as good an explanation as any for why someone might die. That's when Jackson came in with one of his baby blankets. "We can wrap him up in this before we bury him," he said. "But, Mommy, we have to bury him very deep in the snow so that no animals step on him." Except he said it *aMiNals*.

I put on my parka and boots and wrapped Caspar in a paper towel (I had love for the little guy, but not, it turned out, a baby blanket's worth).

"Ready!" I shouted, heading into the living room with Jackson's boots in my hands, admiring how good at dead pets he already was.

"Mommy," he said. "I have an even *better* idea. How about you go and bury him by yourself and I have a little iPad time."

On the coldest day in several years, I went out to the side of our driveway in the almost-dark and lowered him into the hole I made in the snow. I felt the top of Caspar's head, simply for how strange it was to have loved an animal I'd never touched until he was dead. I'd chosen the spot along the driveway because last summer we'd had a toad that visited our porch for bugs every night and this was where a delivery truck had finally squished him. I say I don't believe in God, yet somehow I knew these two bighearted, googly-eyed monsters belonged together, whatever *together* now meant. I say I don't believe in God, but perhaps *this* is the God I believe in: the place where grief and love hold you still.

My husband appeared in the window. The dogs, too. They wagged as they watched me move, as if to say, *Hi there, Heart,* if a dog indeed sees us as its heart walking around outside its body. What did I look like to them now, alone out there, burying a baby frog before our dinner guests arrived? The woman they thought they'd married? A lunatic? Both?

Rest in peace, Caspar Frogpants. You were the best first dead pet my son could ever have had.

At five forty-five a.m. on June 6, 2013, just after the peonies lost their last bloom, Rae Louise Shaw was born in a flash—faster than you can say *inefficient pusher.*

My son was three and a half when my daughter was born—an age, it turns out, that was a particularly tricky one at which to introduce a baby. He was just beginning to separate from us, or, as my husband put it, he was moving from a world of twos into a world of threes. In other words, he was just starting to navigate life beyond the world of *Mother* and *Father,* experimenting with the risky, renegade world of *Others.* And then we dropped a baby on him—and man, oh, man, just like he'd been, was she a scrumptious baby. In retrospect, his response was pretty standard in the land of siblinghood. Or so I hear. He was jealous, mad, loud, sad, anxious. He started throwing things, kicking things. His first nicknames for her were Rae-zilla and the Nothing Doll.

Why can't we all just be dogs? I wanted to know.

Though in 2014, a study out of the University of California, San Diego, concluded that domesticated dogs exhibit this human-grade jealousy, too. (Less is known about the wolf's experience of jealousy, though dogs are such keen social beings it wouldn't surprise me to learn that jealousy is another thing they've absorbed from us.) In an experiment, dogs observed their owners either being affectionate with a stuffed dog (which the dogs viewed as real) or reading a book. Most of them responded to the affection toward the stuffed dog by trying to break it up in various ways, some even with aggression. When we brought baby Safari home, I remember wondering if Booker's initial indifference to him was to be interpreted as jealousy, not rejection. To know a dog, to truly understand a dog, you must be willing to stash away that part of your heart that skews human. You have to, with your human head, feel dog.

While I was, on the one hand, relieved to see Jackson's emotions so vividly—he *wasn't* fine and he was letting us know it—on the other hand, I had no idea what to do with them. They terrified me. As much as I wanted Jackson to have a different experience and *feel* his feelings, I didn't want to be at the other end of them. I didn't know how. And as the home parent, I was the one most often dealing with them. As the mom, I was, too. I'm the one whose body made the baby, after all. And so here I was, five years into married life, nearly four years into motherhood, and my old ways of being the dog had finally caught up with me. Of course they had. Three humans were depending on me to be *Their Person*. Three humans were *My People*. What might have worked when I was a kid no longer worked in a marriage—a good marriage, anyway, a marriage I wanted to keep. When I was a child, being the dog was a harmless and successful survival tactic in my quiet only-child world, but being the dog as an adult was proving avoidant, neglectful even. If the beauty of dogs is that they want to be with you as you are, it's the people who want that, too, who turn the trials of human life into hard-won marvels. And still, dogs and humans can only save you as much as you want to save yourself.

I don't feel like a great mom. Is a good mom enough? Do I need to master emotional honesty to write emotional honesty? Do I forgo the writing or let the kids run our well dry, spraying each other with the hose in great shrieks like cowbells, just so I can finish this sentence?

I couldn't say all of this yet—I knew it and didn't want to know it. But at least I knew enough to press harder into therapy. As difficult as it was to admit, I needed help being a mother because I needed help being me. And it wasn't just the humans who needed me. Booker and his ailing body did. The mighty dog center of our universe was coming to an end. His best friend and brother, Safari, needed me, too.

When Booker started falling and being unable to get up, Safari always stayed by his side. Sometimes I'd look out the window and see them lying out in the grass, two buddies, two lovers of a good scratchy roll in the sun, and not realize they were essentially trapped—Booker by the new limitations of his body, Safari by his unwavering devotion to his friend. Around this same time came the soul-crushing development that Booker lost the ability to wag. But he could still give you those goopy bedroom eyes, and our crushed souls felt fleetingly patched.

A harness was recommended: the Web Master by Ruffwear. This miraculous creation is undoubtedly responsible for giving him his last two years. It didn't prevent him from falling, but it made it so much easier to help him up. He was like a dog suitcase, especially in his last months when I would lift him up and walk him outside and not let him go until we were back at his bed.

In these final years, Safari made his own adjustments. Booker could no longer participate in their long, mouthy, humpy wrestling sessions in the yard, so Safari learned to wrestle with Booker on his bed. He'd walk over, do a little down-dog stretch, and flop down to start licking Booker's mouth. Booker, often on his side, would let the licking run its course, then they'd start what can only be called making out, locking mouths, tongues out, pawing each other playfully. When the session was over, Safari would leave, giving Booker his space until the next bedside visit. I saw something so deep and mutual when coming upon these little visitations. It was like finding children in midwhisper and feeling yourself wanting to know every word they are saying, but also not wanting to break the magic up.

Our house made adjustments. We bought rolls of cheap Home Depot runner to map out the paths Booker regularly walked, as one slip of a toenail on the linoleum or wood could bring him down. Safari seemed to like the rugs because it made things cozier on the floor.

The kids made adjustments, though as kids do, more mysteriously. They were surely taking in all of these other changes— Booker's dramatic falls, Safari's constant concern, all the rugs where there hadn't been rugs before—while not wanting to take in what it all signified: Booker was dying. But, unlike Safari, we could name this for them, explain it with intention and heart. Even though they didn't want to know it, we didn't want their worries to multiply in the devastating eternity of not-knowing.

I'd been down that path before. So we started talking about death. I reminded them of a bird we'd found the previous summer, and of the mice our cats periodically killed in the basement. We likened those stiff little bodies to the soon-to-be-dead body of our resplendent family friend. And when his death did come, when smack in the middle of Safari's Bookie-lit world, Booker the light went out, we surrounded him. We held the dog that now held two dogs. Two hearts. Two essential bodies that, in turn, held mine.

Rae and I were in the car. For a few minutes, I didn't realize NPR was on, which I normally turned off when the kids were with me.

> Rae: Mom, they just said *died*.
> Me: Yes, they did.
> Rae: Buh-ber died.
> Me: Yes, he did.
> Rae: I miss him.
> Me: I do, too.
> Rae: But we still have Safari.
> Me: Yes—and we can think about Booker whenever we want. Do you think about him?
> Rae: No. I just miss him. [A pause.] Is Buh-ber coming back?
> Me: No.
> Rae: Why?
> Me: That's just what happens when you die. Your body goes away. But he's still with us in our minds and hearts.

Rae: I know where he went.

Me: You *do*? *Where?*

Rae: To the aquarium.

Me: Oh! I wonder why he went to the aquarium.

Rae: Because I once saw him turn into a beluga whale.

It was hard for me not to steer the car toward Mystic to see this for myself.

A month later, she was in the middle of her phase of saying unexpected things at check-outs. Things like, "Cat poop," "Diarrhea," and "Mommy tooted." So I felt braced as we neared the front of the line.

"Awww, she's so cute," the cashier said.

"Buh-ber died," Rae replied.

She said it again to a man in the parking lot who told her he liked her boots.

"Buh-ber died."

"Sorry?" he said. "What did she say?"

"We lost our dog Booker earlier this summer," I explained. "She's been telling everybody."

It was true. It had become her greeting, and I was a little jealous, because I realized that was what *I* wanted to say to everybody. It was all I'd wanted to say all summer. To the garbageman: Booker died; to my son's summer camp counselor: Booker died; to my dentist: Booker died; to the last black rhino on earth: *Booker died*.

It's the permanence of loss, of course, that makes it so unbearable. But it's also the loneliness. It feels wrong to be so distraught over an animal. It feels childish. He was *just a dog*. Only he wasn't just a dog. No dog is, if you listen to what they are telling you. If you see what they offer in the dark. A dog is a trampoline park three hundred feet off the highway. A dog is a swift kiss in the rain. A dog is, to steal a line from Stephen Dobyns, "the answer to what comes next and how to like it."

What a thing it would be always to say what we really want to say. Not "I'm fine," but "I'm terrified." Not "I'm fine," but "I'm lost." Not "I'm fine," but "I'm in pain." My grandfather Seaweed always hated when people told him to "have a nice day!" He thought he should be able to have any kind of day he wanted. And he was right. I'd love to spend a day saying exactly what I want to say, saying the words over and over until I feel understood, like any reasonable two-year-old.

Despite my two-dog theory and the idea that Booker would live on in a whole lifeline of dogs like those hand-in-hand paper doll chains you cut as a kid, it took even me almost a year before I started thinking about that next dog, the one that Safari would infuse with Booker, and himself, the one they would all live on in. I was undoubtedly mourning, but I was also that much more smitten with Safari, who was living the only-dog life quite beautifully. In fact, without his comrade, his armor, his trusty canine crutch, he was more self-embodied than ever. Booker and Safari were such a tight twosome and Booker had shaped so much of who Safari had become, it had always been hard to consider them separately—the same way Harriet and I spent so much time together as children that instead of saying, "Hi, Chloe," people would often greet me with, "Where's Harriet?" when encountering me without her. The presence of either Booker or Safari immediately called to mind the absence of the other. But as we settled into our life with one dog, Safari boldly cut through that reflex. He was present. He was steady. He was calm. It really was as if he knew he was now living for both of them—and as if he'd finally learned that he alone was enough. He saw the Booker-shaped hole in our hearts and wiggled in.

While one day considering this regal transformation, I looked up the name his rescue had given him: Matsi. It means "sweet and brave" and was the name of the beta wolf in the captive Saw-tooth Pack, made famous through the work of Jim Dutcher in 1990s Idaho. Matsi was second in the hierarchy, as well as the peacemaker and puppy sitter. While I only know him as Safari now, it stuns me how perfect this original name really was. Safari is simply the sweetest thing there is. He approaches children, even feral ones, as if they're all made of eggshell, sniffing them, licking them with the Zen energy of the final moments of a yoga class. He looks into their faces as if some part of them is his own. And you can call him fearful for his many fears, but for his many fears you can also call him brave. It takes a vast amount of courage to face each day when it's the basic makings of a day you fear most. Noise, movement, people. His eyeing the world with such un-certainty and dread and then going out in it anyway is not only the greatest act of bravery I get to witness every day, it's how I do it myself.

I know nothing about the first four months of Safari's life, but I have a vision of it, anyway. He's sitting in an overgrown, rural backyard contentedly, like Ferdinand, perhaps, quietly, just smelling the flowers. All around him, his siblings, and maybe some other dogs and animals, sleep and play and muck about.

He doesn't join them but sits where he is, happy to be alive and watching, pleased to be who and where he is on the periphery, striking the beveled edge of where life gets made. I know nothing about the day he was born, but that he was born in my heart.

My Fears

Safari's Fears

War
Raisins in Baked Goods
Aluminum Foil
Flying
Hitchcock
Squirrels
Blimps
Fire
Flying Hubcaps
Kurt Cobain
Lightning
Domestic Chores
Being Buried Alive
The Twilight Zone
Spinning
The Grim Reaper
Drooling
Soup Samples
Flying Mammals
Splitting My Pants
Clowns

Wind
Death
Eating
Compartmentalization
Heights
Birds
Conflict
Blimpies
Burning Man
Decapitation
Anger
Collaboration
Failure
Shovels
Talking Toys
Heli-Propulsion
Hoods
Cujo
Tiny Cups
Speed
Dancing
Frozen Faces

Trucks
Metal Bowls
Plastic Bags
Being Carried
Birds
Words
Sandwiches
People
Frisbees
Vacuums
Thunder
Puppy Kindergarten
Humans
Toys
Big-Ass Fans
Range Hoods
Rabies
Urine Samples
Sneezing
Eye Contact
The Chill Mockery of Cats

The Dog House

Out on the screened porch, the dogs have joined me. Otter's nose twists around right up against the screen toward all the new smells the crepuscular yard goings-on left for him. Safari sends his nose up, too, but from the center of the room, where I am. He likes to stay close to me. Tickling between his ears, I plant my feet firmly on the warm wood and try to glimpse an animal in the woods. There's always something out there uprooting the moss, nibbling the berries.

Like the angle of the sun, the appearance of certain animals in our yard often tells me the time of day, and year. Bobcats, coyotes, foxes, raccoons, cats, groundhogs, deer, turkeys, skunks, bats, owls, fireflies. This hour of summer mornings, it's birds. From the long porch table, I can hear them but cannot see them, except for the hummingbirds in their big, looping fights for the feeder. One makes a deep arc the size of a tugboat and the other leaves. As for the rest of the birds of North America, they're in the trees for now. Later, their shadows will ripple across the lawn and porch floor like the trembling shadows of fish moving several feet under the water.

Same as my dogs, my wild animal visitors have a knack for cutting right through the torn, lonely parts of me. As my solitude over the week set in, and the unrelenting anxieties that have moored me my whole life rose up through my veins like squid ink, the sight of a pair of coyotes jetting through the back splash of our yard flushes the Fear of Everything back down. Wild things in their wild place have always reassured me. Their wildness makes the wildness within me feel less wild. I feel more capable of setting aside the tedious, old ways of worry to set the teakettle instead, to shop for a week's worth of groceries that no one other than I need enjoy, to do a miraculous load of laundry for one. Without the company of wild things, I feel more likely to step out into the yard and take up that wild role myself, and who knows what might happen then. The coyotes come so I can stay inside, *Me*—the Me at least I've always known best, not always fully human herself.

Though I am alone here, I am *home*, so the house has others' stories to tell. My family is nearly four hundred miles away, eating burgers by a pool, attending clay camp, catching up on psychoanalytic reading, and romping around Rochester with extended family, but their things are here with me. In the absence of my three, I am surrounded by them. My children's rooster and dragonfly drawings, their sculptures of Neymar and Otter; my husband's shoes in the mudroom with their prickled green beards, last worn in the yard just after the grass was cut; our shelf of chaos in the kitchen—keys, strings, hair ties, pens, cups, rulers, fidget spinners, soap; a blond hair in the sink. I see broken headphones on the couch where my son left them before heading out one week ago, exchanging them for a new working set last-minute, even though his father and I were chanting, *Get in the car get in the car get in the car.* I see the Blanket-with-a-capital-B my daughter mistakenly left on the kitchen chair and—in the tones and tears of an emergency—wished she hadn't one hour into the drive north. I spend a moment staring at it, wishing I had Jeannie's power and could twitch-my-nose it to her, drop it directly into her delighted, small hands. I intentionally left the dirty sheets on the bed because they smell like my husband, like us, but I did spend some time tidying up. I know myself well enough to know that I need a good, clear space in which to think.

I stand in the yard and watch Safari unbury his favorite broken tennis ball out from under the leaves and weeds among a nearby patch of woods, trotting it out gleefully to the center of the yard, dropping it in front of him with a downward-dog bow, lying before it as if in worship, as if this jagged neon flap reveals a piece of life's mystery. After a few minutes, he carries it gently back to the same area, digs a new hole, and buries it again, this rotten, holy treasure, his nose nudging new soil over it. Otter watches Safari's doting practice like a hunting dog on point, holding his own newer, intact ball in his mouth like a security blanket. He always watches Safari, eleven years his elder, with a kind of fixed reverence, a most earnest curiosity, until distracted by some other source of life—the piercing chirps of chipmunks crying out from the old rock property-line wall or the shadows of birds, which he chases, not thinking to look up at the source when there's something so fantastic down. When I skew my vision enough to shift the dogs into fuzzier focus, it truly is as if Booker never left. Otter's great big chocolatey body could easily pass for Booker's out on the grass any day. He even has the same circular windmill wag that clears lower tables. It was never the intention when we chose Otter—and, to be clear, Otter is as ridiculous as Booker was regal—but he's surely and shockingly grown into a stockier, shorter-nosed version of him. I wonder how they would have done together—but I know. They would have had a ball. Maybe two.

In the middle of the ache of this, I feel the brief tremor of something other than broken. I take a moment to remember Booker's death for how we managed it—as dutifully as we'd managed his life. I feel moved, watching Otter and Safari contemplate grass, by all we did to help that dear heartsnap of a dog on his way. Booker was like the Mick Jagger of dogs—he had groupies, a shameless, devoted following—so in the months and weeks leading up to this day, I made sure to tell his groupies so his groupies could gather, a final tribute. One by one, with tissues, they came. Lauren, Kyla, Erin, Beth, Kira, and Dee. They sat by his bed, put hands to his body, said goodbye to the dog it seemed only love had made. I know he didn't understand the goodbye of it all—goodbyes are another human contrivance around which dogs must begrudgingly bend—but he did understand the love in these faces and voices because he was part of it. Even in death, as they remembered him, he remembered them.

While the grief I'd been feeling was blinding, I was starting to wonder if the grief itself was starting to feel okay. *Where in a body does grief you dare not speak of go?* Perhaps, nowhere. Perhaps that is what grief is supposed to do—it sets up its thriving camp and never leaves. And perhaps the object isn't to destroy it after all, but bring it dogs and maps for when the winter road clears.

Back inside the screened porch, they sleep, two worn-out floofs, Safari in the sun on the rug, Otter by my foot. I read and eat breakfast, Otter's warm gorilla chest pushing against my ankle as he breathes. Occasionally, he will dream, or will seem to anyway, his floppy, furry paws going up and down in sync with his eyebrows. His pink bubblegum tongue often sticks out when he sleeps and even for the first few minutes after he wakes. It seems to me one of his doggiest moments as a dog, if to be a dog is to live wholly in the present without the burden of judgment and self-loathing. If to be a dog is to be so boldly oneself—trembling, howling, unequivocal. He has absolutely no awareness of how ridiculous he looks, or what ridiculousness *is*, and so ridiculousness doesn't exist. My dogs have no way to gauge how much I love them other than food and the fact that when I leave, I always come back to scratch and kiss all over them, saying, "Heyyyyyyyyyy, boo boos. You're *such* boo boos." What am I without my humans? Still human? Or some other creature I have yet to know? "I am because my little dog knows me," writes Gertrude Stein. For the moment, anyway, I am merely everything before me. I am light. I am leaves. I am dog. I am air.

What are you, Dog? How can you lie on my foot, then act like you've never seen a foot before when I go to stand? Do you mislead me? I, you? Would you enjoy wearing a sweater? Or would you prefer to eat me? Do you see the things I see? Do you know me? Do you care? Am I right that unlike human silence, your silence doesn't have rage in it? Does your language include one or twenty words for despair? Is it easier to accept love when you don't know the word love? *Or do you know it? Have you known it all along? Does the aching greenness of words never spoken slow your blood to mud, too? Am I any closer to whole forty years later, lying here, still being the dog whenever the rest feels too big? Do you know the meaning of things, how one thing can lead to another—that beneath these words I type there is this table, then the bench, then the window frame, then the screen, then the hedges, then the dandelions shooting up our old grass, then the Japanese maples, then the space where the hammock was mysteriously cut in two that day Safari brought me a skull from the woods, then the spot where the tiny pine cones drop, the helicoptering maple seeds, too, then the spot where Booker, the dog you never knew but must still smell in our teeth somewhere, lay dead atop the moving blanket we buried him in, then his crackly bones, his paw pads, and the mothered-up, ruffled rest of him? Do you know you'll die one day, too, Dog? Like him, you will carry the light long after we've walked you to the woods. We will remember you. How we held you in our hands.*

Otter: Dog of Reckoning

(2018–present)

Haiku for the Dog
You could eat me if
You wanted to, but you don't.
Want to, that is. Right?

When we open ourselves to the possibility of love, we open ourselves to the possibility of breaking; when we open ourselves to the possibility of breaking, we open ourselves to the possibility of being made whole again. Almost one year after Booker died, we adopted Otter—part Catahoula leopard dog, part Irish setter mix, and part otter, it seemed. That mound of fuzzy head. During another Petfinder binge, I found his tiny half-speckled face—a puppy Phantom of the Opera. His name was Knight and he lived in Jackson, Tennessee. When I spoke to his foster mom, Carol, on the phone, she told me he was so small that she had to watch for hawks when she let the puppies out of the barn for fresh air. After we'd officially adopted him, he came north one night on a truck full of puppies and dogs and I drove to a nearby horse farm to pick him up. All the humans gathered at the truck door, and one by one they brought the puppies out. "Knight!" a man finally said, holding him up in the air. The whole crowd cooed at how adorable he was. He reminded me of the first illustration of Wilbur in *Charlotte's Web*. Ears back, eyes wide and vulnerable, belly out. His little body, partly coated in dry poop, went completely stiff, the way animals freeze in the face of uncertainty. I walked up and took him in my arms and brought his face to my face. It took a minute, then his whole body wagged. This struck me as a remarkable moment in a dog's life—and proof to me that dogs are optimists. His glass half full, he took me as a good thing—my glass half dog—and a good thing I would remain, unless, of course, I proved to be a bad thing.

At his first vet visit, Heather told him, "You've got some big paws to fill, mister." She was right. But, oh, my kids were at such sweet ages for a puppy—four and seven. Though, like adopting Safari, Otter was my idea (or my stubborn, even selfish, insistence, I can say now), my husband *was* making a sound when petting him I hadn't heard him make since Booker died. A soft, low *hmmhmmhmm* accompanied by scratches behind the ears. But what was most moving was seeing Safari act as pack leader. I was watching my dog-lineage vision play out perfectly. Safari, who was raised by Booker, was raising Otter now. As with Booker, it took a little while for Safari to warm up. When I first introduced him to his new little brother (I presented him with what I imagined would be of most interest: Otter's back end), he took one sniff and turned his head away in what can only be described as doggie disgust. He even did this to me when he could smell the puppy all over my clothes and hands. But I gave Safari his space and time and he slowly opened up to Otter on his own terms. He started tracking Otter around the yard and initiating play with him. Otter looked as happy as the little kid on the playground who finally gets the big kid's attention. Since Safari still had his limits, which would be delivered in quick, growly bursts, Otter had to learn restraint. It was like watching Robin Williams try to restrain himself before a lit crowd. Just like Booker taught Safari, Safari taught Otter all the dog stuff, too. *This is where you pee. This is when you bark. Enough is enough and get out of my face already.* I could see it happening before me and felt Booker there, too, maybe one step ahead of Safari, as Safari ran maybe one step ahead of Otter, who ran maybe one step ahead of the trail of dogs yet to come—but all of whom would always be following that first one, Booker the swashbuckler, the cinnamon roll, the sound of Sunday leaping deep in the woods. Eyebrows. Legs. Black-spotted tongue of wonder. Otter has a black spot on his tongue, too.

Though as much as Safari shaped the dog Otter is, they are supremely different beings, operating as differently inside the house as out. Safari, the gentle soul, seeks out in his downtime the quiet corners in which to perch. He likes to curtail any possibility of something sneaking up on him. Otter, on the other hand, is all in all the time. He wants to be where the action is, where the people are, where life most boldly buzzes. "Otter's the happiest dog in the world," Jackson likes to say. I always wonder if in this there is a tinge of me at his age—that this is his wanting to be the dog. But happy is right. When he greets someone his whole body wriggles with the same absurd theatrics as Steve Martin and Dan Aykroyd's Two Wild and Crazy Guys. And when I say "someone" I mean everyone, anyone. His excitement is like a Ping-Pong ball let loose in a glass house.

His facial expressions, too, are fantastically revealing. A lovely psychologist I know who works with children has a bowl filled with slips of paper on which she has written an enormous array of emotions. *Worried. Happy. Scared. Frustrated.* She asks patients to pick out the ones they have felt that day to demonstrate how many feelings we can legitimately feel—even simultaneously. If she asked Otter to do this exercise, I am certain he would pull out every last one. If humans have twenty-seven different emotions, Otter has at least one hundred forty-nine. He seems to run through the entire course of them hourly. He is fantastically sensitive, responding to voice, action, and light with equal enthusiasm. While Safari merely pretends to have a genetic predisposition to chewing bones, Otter receives such toys as if Santa himself is handing them over. He gently takes them in his teeth, and his ears go limp as if he's overwhelmed at deserving such an honor, and he does little wags like he's the luckiest dog on Earth but he doesn't want to celebrate so much that it seems braggy.

Otter always seems to be saying, *YES!! ME!!* before he even knows what is involved. The only things that give him pause are watching me pick up his poop, which he does with a combination of pity and despair, and encountering something new, something that wasn't there before. If he happens upon a room with rearranged furniture, he freezes in the face of Something Different and growls. "It's okay," I say, walking over to it so he can, too. He always wags at the revelation and comes closer to sniff. He once had a ten-minute early-morning standoff with a chair I'd moved to the center of the patio for a self-timed picture of the kids and me the afternoon before. He had the same thing with a neighbor's statue of Mary.

He's that dog who always greets you with a toy in his mouth, that dog who believes he's far smaller than he is, backing up into any lap that's available—even the crisscross-applesauced legs of a small child—that dog who doesn't want to be just close to you but touching, until he falls into a sleep so deep he forgets who and where and that he *is*. And when he sleeps, he sticks his tongue out and farts like a human. As much as he's grown to resemble Booker, he's less secure, more sensitive, harder to settle. Sometimes it seems he heads into his crate just to turn his brain off. Makes sense to me. The world for some is way too much. If there were such a thing as canine cannabis, I'd be happy to light up his doobie or send him out for a night with that *Dazed and Confused* breed of McConaughey.

In order to stave off an overwhelmed puppy-burdened household scenario, I'd taken full responsibility for Otter from the beginning. This was nothing new. I'm already—and happily—the full-time animal caretaker here, but I took on this puppy with a kind of vengeance I regret. This was mostly due to the emotional climate we were in. The truth is, Matt hadn't wanted this dog—or he hadn't wanted *just* this dog. What he still wanted was *me*. And so because I was still in a place where being *me* felt too hard, I pushed hard again for the *dog* me, not the human me. It was guilt now driving me to make it appear that we'd never actually gotten Otter. Rather than listening to what Matt was telling me—*I see you, I love you, I hold you*—I, the first zero-trace human, set out to raise the first zero-trace puppy. I'd make a two-dog household feel like a one-dog household if it killed me. I popped up at two a.m. for the puppy let-outs before Matt could hear a squeak. I fed him and walked him and took him to puppy kindergarten and the vet and made all the decisions about him without saying a word. On the one hand, I was proud of his training and that I'd successfully attached him to his crate (I'd never crate-trained a dog before). But on the other, my global responsibility for him started to have an unexpected and undesirable effect. His complete trust in me seemed to be making him less trusting of others. He acted more anxiously around Matt and the kids, jumping up if they passed by him when he was resting, or tensely licking their hands. He had trouble settling into the mix comfortably, though he clearly *wanted* to be in the mix. We'd only had dogs you could lie on top of, dogs who practically nannied the kids, so it made me nervous to see him respond to his own family this way. He was the kids' first puppy—he was their Agatha—but it was their frenetic energy that put him most on edge. He suddenly felt more complicated than cute; I felt alone and deflated.

As is par for the course with rescue dogs, I know so little about his first two months. But one thing Carol told me came to mind. In our last conversation before he was driven north, she said, "Well, I hope you're ready to love this little boy right up, because I took him to get fixed today and now he won't even look at me. He's one sensitive little guy." We laughed and I said, "Of course I am." I can't imagine seventeen straight hours in a truck full of dogs and puppies did *nothing* to inform a sensitive little guy either. Whatever it was, I seemed to miss some of the particulars of this sensitivity as he formed from puppy to dog. How much he would have benefited from our whole family's being more involved. I completely understand that not everyone likes dog licks and big waggy, shaggy bodies all over the place. Though they love dogs, Matt and the kids tend to fall in that category, and so, naturally, sometimes push him away, especially when he's being a big puppy who just wants *in*. I'm the opposite. I'm the only one who never pushes him away. There's never a time—unless someone else's comfort or discomfort is involved—when I give him the message *Go away, dog*. Now we had to desensitize him to the same hands and feet he called home. We as a family had to learn to use words more, bodies less, to direct him. The children already knew this lesson well, of course. After all, it was the same way we were raising them. *Use your words*, we were always saying. We had to train him to trust his family again, and it felt like my fault. I'd brought home a dog again to avoid *me*—yet by this point, I'd unwittingly already become more unavoidably me than ever.

Halfway into my forty-third year, I arrived at that place in my therapy I'd long fought to avoid. I couldn't stop crying. I'd certainly cried in therapy before, but I mean I was crying most of the session, every time. I wasn't relying on the things I used to anymore—though I still had dogs, I'd become too close to my humanness to know anymore how to *be* them, or really to *need* to be them. There was just being, and it was hard. I cried at home after I put the kids to bed and whenever my husband looked at me and said, "You've been on my mind." He would come toward me and instead of turning into him, I'd curl away and into myself. I wanted so much to be someone, something—anything—else. I wanted to be out of my body again, flung off, or down inside the dog. I wanted something to hold me so I didn't have to hold myself. I knew enough to know this likely meant something significant—progress, process, movement—but the pain I felt was near debilitating. Old pain, new pain, pain of old pain crashing into new pain. Pain of everything lost or broken; pain of secrets and fears; of all there is to be done; of the impossible task of knowing what is pain, what is love, what is real; of all the words I never said now puffed up like manatees inside my chest. It was as if I were feeling *Everything* for the first time.

Otter had come home in the middle of my darkest place—of our darkest. Did he know? Like the geraniums in *E. T.*, was his anxiety reflecting my own? Therapy had been life-giving, but the true process of it (even when you're not in an analysis) can be lengthy, lifelong. I was still in the process of breaking down, of breaking systems down, systems that had formed me, systems I had relied on since before I knew the word *system*, systems that might have helped in childhood but were failing me as an adult. And what about my body that I'd gone in and out of for so long? *Yes, no; human, dog.* What would be there to hold up my healing heart and head? Seven years into parenthood, nine years into marriage, twenty-five years into writing, forty-three years into a body, and nothing felt particularly good. In the mirror, I only saw the myriad tolls of pregnancy and early motherhood. Inside, my heart was bleak. And a dog is a reliable companion inside a bleak heart, but not the way out of it—not a lasting way. While a marvel, a dog's empathy only goes so far. I've had the experience of crying with a dog only to feel more alone, because while you lie searching for the shiny thing, to a dog, you'll always be the thing that's shiny.

And so it was within this sticky climate during the bustle of breakfast and coats and kids one morning that I took Otter into the yard and threw the ball for him. Though I throw the ball far and long, I always keep a twenty-foot leash on him in case I need to grab him quick if he, say, sees a squirrel or heads toward the road.

I took turns throwing the tennis ball and kicking his favorite old soccer ball, which he is extraordinary in maneuvering. A regular canine Salah, I tell you. I was just having the thought that he was doing so great with me back there, so focused on *here* and *ball* and not on running away the way some dogs are the minute the opportunity arises, like a friend's dog who runs away so often he wears a GPS. *Freedom! Smells! Nine hundred thousand feet of fucking air!* I let the tennis ball go and just at the peak of its arc, I saw what Otter was seeing, and that was not the ball but a large buck that hadn't been there a few seconds before. It appeared that I'd thrown the ball directly where the buck was standing, so it was already on the run, and so was Otter, his brain having shifted from *Ball!* to *HolyshitwhatthefuckisthatIneedthepanickedrunningthinginmymouthrightnow!* He was off, back into the woods like a fuzzy missile. The deer was way ahead, but no matter. They both disappeared behind the neighbor's broken fence at the back of our property. I called, *Otter, come!* a million times, the way I'd taught him in puppy kindergarten. He'd even earned a diploma for it. He was supposed to have good enough recall so that I could call him off a situation like this, and his recall *is* good, but not, as it turns out, *deer* good. I called and called, thinking, *At least he went back toward the woods and not toward the road. But if he keeps going he will hit a road.*

Matt appeared along the old rock wall at the end of our driveway. He didn't ask what had happened or say anything, he just began to call Otter, too. I teared up watching him standing there calling like I was. We were suddenly together here. And that hadn't been the feeling around this dog for a while now. It shouldn't have been a surprise to me, but I was acting like it was. Why had I expected Matt suddenly to become as much of a dog-needer as I was when he'd never been a dog-needer—not even with Booker? He loved Booker, learned from Booker, Booker was undoubtedly (and always would be) part of his soul, but the loss of that dog didn't translate into his needing another. For him, I believe knowing Booker could have sufficed as a spectacular, singular experience. He had asked for more space for us humans and I kept adding dogs.

My daughter came out and called, too. I told them about the deer, then went inside for a package of sausage I could crinkle. I got boots on for the woods.

It was time for my husband to take the kids to school, but they lingered in the driveway in the discomfort of departing with the situation unresolved—and perhaps, too, at the parting visual of their mother, heading into the woods in her nightgown, sweatpants, rain boots, and winter coat with the hood pulled on, with a package of sausages in her hand. (The absurdity of it reminded me of the snipe hunts my Texas grandparents, Mudder and Daddy-D, used to take my cousins and me on. In order to find the elusive snipe, we were instructed to enter a field at night and lightly beat a hanger inside a pillowcase. The adults would stand around us with flashlights and cheer us on. Needless to say, we never found one.)

"Love you guys!" I called, thinking, *I might not* look *normal, but I can sound normal.*

After they'd disappeared down the driveway, I went around to the left, where the neighbor's fence was down and where I'd seen the deer and Otter go, but there was nothing, so I went to the back right of our property, where there was better access to the big stretch of woods along the brook down there. I was thankful for the bed of crunchy leaves because I thought even if I couldn't see him, I might hear him crunching along like an elephant, the way everything sounds bigger than itself in the fall. Chipmunks become dire wolves. But even when I stopped down by the water, even when all I did was listen, I heard nothing in the woods, only the distant *whoosh whoosh whoosh* of cars at rush hour.

Maybe they'll see him on the way to school, I thought. *Maybe they'll see him dead on the road. Maybe they'll hit him.*

I looked out at the woods. He couldn't have gone *that* far. I worried about the leash he was still attached to, that it would get stuck on something and we wouldn't find him and he'd die like that in the woods, terrified, stuck at the end of his stuck leash. I spent about twenty minutes back there, walking, stopping, calling, walking, stopping, calling.

What if this is it? What if we never see him again? What if I have to tell the kids? Would they care?

My stomach, a dragon fruit.

As I sat down to compose my lost-dog post, my phone rang. It was a local number I didn't know. I never answer calls from numbers I don't know. I picked up immediately.

"Hello?" I said.

"Hi. Uhhh. I have Otter?"

Even though the caller was around the bend, three doors down a different road, our yards touched at the corners.

I pulled up to the house and thought how happy-wiggly Otter would be to see me, how this man would get to see the sweeping love between Woman and Dog. And he *was* happy when the man, who was wearing a hoodie over what I imagined was still early-morning hair, led him around the corner to me, but not overly so. He almost looked a bit deflated, confused, as if thinking, *What? This is over? I was just getting started here! There was that panicked thing, a speedy scenario through the woods, a fuckload of sniffing, this new guy here. It can't be over. We can't be going* home. *What about* this *guy? What if I prefer how this guy smells?*

I thanked the man profusely, opened the trunk for Otter to hop up, and drove home, realizing halfway that I had never gotten the man's name. I also realized I was shaking.

Thirty minutes later, my husband called. He hadn't seen my text telling him Otter was safe at home.

"I imagine you're feeling rattled," he said. "What a morning. I've been thinking about you."

I started sobbing and trying to talk through the sobbing about how I regretted getting Otter, that I felt bad that no one else seemed to love him like I did, or to *want* to love him. I was finally feeling the selfish side of adding dogs to a house that might have been happier, calmer, easier without them, adding dogs to a house that only needed me.

"You know I wasn't happy the way we got him," he said. "Just like when we got Safari. I wasn't happy where *we* were. But he's a great dog. He's *our* dog. It's going to be okay."

I was pacing the house as I always do when on the phone, stopping in front of the portraits I'd had made of Booker and Safari several years ago by a man I found in an aphasia video I was watching for research. He lived in Virginia, and though a traumatic brain injury had left him unable to form words on his tongue, he could draw and paint beautifully. He especially loved to paint animals, someone in the video said, so I found him on Etsy. The portraits hang in our living room, and they caught my attention just then because of how much the Booker portrait looked like Otter, like he was already a little bit here before we knew him, before he was born, even, our little spotted misfit of Jackson, Tennessee.

It's going to be okay.

"I thought I could love him for all four of us," I told Matt. "But love doesn't work like that, does it?"

"Nope," he said. "I love him and I love you."

"I love him and I love you, too," I said, understanding a little better where we were but not necessarily knowing what to do about it.

10th Anniversary for Matt

14 June 2018

You who appeared in the woods one day,
As if to say,
Wolves matter,
But your teeth are human teeth.
Hear that heart?
Human.
Be upright with me for a bit;
You can always crawl if needed.
I can't promise comfort,
But something undeniable;
A wolf's pain settles wholly in the eyes.
I will hunt,
And haunt.
I will eat parts of you,
Brace for parts of me to be eaten.

I will stoop to clear the rocks from your eyes,
Then pelt you with them in your sleep.
Stay anyway.
Stay 'til the wolves even seem more human—
Dogs.

My father-in-law has been losing his memory probably since before I knew him. Like lots of dementias, it has crept up and over like a slow, steady weed, not even visible at its beginning— too crowded in by the beauty of the blooms that were his uncommon decency, work ethic, and propensity to twinkle. When I met him thirteen years ago, it's possible we were already at, or through, the beginning, though it's hard to know. He's been in chronic pain ever since breaking his back in his first college football game. Even so, he's lived a big life right through it. He's been happily married for more than fifty years, raised three boys into men, and ran his family's steel business for decades. He's been a loyal friend and father and has always been the one most concerned with how everyone in the room is feeling. But this last bunch of years, we've watched him disappear behind big, blinking eyes and a thin frame. He's quieter, more internal. And when he talks, he doesn't always make sense. He doesn't always know who we are. But he's not angry about it. He's scared and frustrated but relatively happy for someone slipping into obscurity. At this stage, it seems much harder on my mother-in-law, his caretaker and sweetheart since they were fifteen.

If you know one person with dementia, the doctor told her, you know one person with dementia. Papa is our one person. His terror and bewilderment are our own, though that's not entirely true, is it? We remember Florida and dolphins and each other. We don't peer out from our eyes and see giraffe-shaped holes where giraffes once were. When we sit with him on his bed, scanning the sea for dolphins, I'm not sure he can picture what a dolphin is, but he is looking, going through the motions, hopeful, perhaps, that he'll know a dolphin when he sees one.

"Now, who are you again?" he said to me on our annual visit to Siesta Key as he tickled Rae, flashing her his big, old panda smile.

Remember me.

"I'm Chloe," I said. "I'm married to your son Matt."

"And where is he?"

"Right there."

"Hey, Papa." Matt waved.

"Sorry I'm so dumb," Papa said.

"Not *dumb*!" Jackson yelled at him. Third grade had taught him well. "You're funny and forgetful, is what you are."

"Thanks, Tommy," Papa said.

He was making a joke. I'm not sure he could have said Jackson's correct name, but he'd been using random names as intentional wrong ones. It was very clever. The air split open with laughter.

"What are you laughing at, Mary?" he said to Rae.

He was on a roll.

A little later, he surprised all of us, turning to me, asking, "Do you have any dogs?"

"We have two—Safari and Otter. We used to have Booker, who was your favorite. Everyone's favorite, really. You used to sit in a chair and Safari would get on one side of you and Booker on the other. They'd back up into you so you could scratch their backs with each of your hands. You'd do this all day if you could, but eventually you'd have so much dog hair on your hands and lap—tumbleweeds of it rolling across the floor—that Mimi would gently urge you to stop. You know what else, Papa? Your boys used to call you Barn Dog. Barn Dog would tie on a red bandana and go biking around the lake."

Remember me.

I had a vision of him near death in a hospital bed, his hands down at each side, pantomiming this beloved act against the backs of ghost dogs, the way my grandfather Daddy-D, in his last days, obliviously mimed smoking cigarettes.

When not out sharing a meal with us, or sitting by the pool watching the kids swim, he stayed in his bed with his sizable stack of sudoku. He slept. We noticed that once the sun went down, he was worse. He sometimes wandered out of his room in his pajamas a couple of hours after having gone to bed, picking up objects from the rental apartment, asking us when we were going to return these things to the people they belonged to. My mother-in-law would calmly usher him back to bed.

While so much else has fallen away, it's clear that love is the thing that Papa remembers best.

"I don't know what I'd do without her," he says multiple times a day. "She's so nice to me."

"Well, you've been so nice to her, Papa," we tell him.

On our last night, over the deepest bowls of vanilla ice cream you've ever seen, Papa leaned in close to me and squeezed my hand.

"My family is going to be here any minute," that tender old dog told me. "And I think you're going to *love* them."

Somewhere beneath the sun-spotted dome of his head, I heard one thousand miniature crabs click-clacking in opposite directions.

"Now," he said. "*Who* are you again?"

"I'm Chloe, Papa. Chloe."

I said it twice because it felt good to be Chloe the Person this time.

Remember me.

My daughter has a book called *Princess Hyacinth: The Surprising Tale of a Girl Who Floated*. It tells the tale of a princess who's unable to stay on the ground unless weights are tucked into her gown and crown, and it was she who came into my mind as I thought about this development with Otter that had brought me so fully back into my body—into Chloe the Person—after so many decades of wanting out, and the tough reality to which I'd finally conceded, that this dog whom I'd demanded had become, as if himself a fur-lined intervention, the most demanding of me. Now that I knew this, how to, like a dog but as my best human self, sit here in my body and *stay*? How not to go dog again, how not to float away? What weights could I tuck into *my* gown and crown? Then one day I had my answer: kettlebells.

I'd heard about Christa Doran and her gym, Tuff Girl Fitness, for a few years but had yet to find my way to her. I was too scared. Too floating. Too dog. But if one thing separates Woman from Beast, it's the iron-braised swing of a kettlebell.

New Haven is a small-town city. If we are all six degrees of separation away from Kevin Bacon, I'd bet that many residents of the greater New Haven area are even fewer away from Tuff

Girl. It isn't a typical gym. You work out in a group—usually all women, though men are welcome and do occasionally pop in. You can spot Tuff Girls out in the world by what might be the gang signs of the fitness world: their logo. Picture the classic ladies' bathroom symbol but with a dumbbell in her hand. I'd seen for myself the women who worked out there—all different shapes and ages—and they were *strong*, the most common trait among them: Quads! Shoulders! Whatever went on there was clearly way too badass for me. *Me*—the only child who never caused a stir, who stayed the steady course at *fine*. I thought an argument meant the end of a relationship, *forever*. I liked a good 5K to embarrassing music, not audibly grunting during workouts you're encouraged to "crush." (At least I didn't think I did.) Instead I thought, *commitment* and *group*. It's a gym that runs *classes*, which means you have to *sign up*, which means you have to *sign over your name* and work out *with other people*, which means *people*. Those muscles, though. I wanted them. And I was so tired of floating. Of hiding in the close hazy shave of the stratus clouds. So, bright and early one Saturday morning, I drove to Hamden and crossed the hallowed threshold, hoping to infuse my bad kind of tough with the good kind of tuff.

How to describe opening the door to Tuff Girl? It's like stepping off an iceberg straight into the middle of a party. It's like shifting from black and white into every color there is. It's sound! It's sweat! It's life! And it might as well be the set of *Cheers*, because when you walk through the door—yes, I'm really gonna say it—everybody knows your name. This door isn't just a door, we are often reminded. It's the threshold between the rest of our lives and the hour that we are here. The door holds the stories at Tuff Girl.

"Are you Chloe?" A woman walked up and shook my hand. "I'm Christa."

I'd have been hard-pressed to come up with a more seamless union of radiance and strength. What a happy life I could have had as just one of her shoulders.

She told me that she was glad I had come and asked if there was anything she should know about my body—aches, pains, injuries, surgeries. I mentioned two shoulder surgeries but stopped short of detailing my life as a dog.

I signed in on the tablet and found a cubby while staying clear of the turf—a long, narrow slice of Astroturf snug up against the black gym floor—since sleds weighing two hundred and sixty pounds or more were still being pushed at a pace that would have put Iditarod pups to shame. Then the controlled chaos between classes began. Coats, water bottles, hugs, high fives, keys, kisses.

While I waited for the blacktop to clear, a picture on the wall got my attention: a girl, maybe four years old, in a bathing suit, her face tilted up toward the pouring rain, her eyes squeezed shut as she seemed to scream with an exhilarating, even ferocious joy—an ecstatic release, to be certain. "Remember her?" it said in white type across her belly. I stood there staring. No, I sure didn't. I was never that girl. I can't tell you of a single time (before having kids) when I yelled—out of joy or agony or anger. The only relief I had as I stood there was in realizing that though the little girl in no way reminded me of myself, she reminded me *very* much of my daughter when she closed her eyes, tilted her face up, and belted out Alicia Keys's "Girl on Fire."

I walked out onto the blacktop and lay down for warm-up. *Leave everything at the door.* That day, I left: a husband packing for a funeral; two sick, cabin-fevered kids; two fighting cats; two big dogs who could have used more exercise that day if it weren't for the torrents out there; a broken dishwasher; the three a.m. fear that our house would catch fire, that my children would remember me as unhappy, that they would *be* unhappy, that the planets will lose their rotation and we will all be sent hurtling into the sun. And this was when Coach Karin told me to breathe. And this is when I breathed. What a happy life I could have had as just one of her legs.

That body that was so agonizing to be in, to want to stay in? Not anymore. I was finally not only fully inhabiting my human body but indulging in it, pushing it, using it for everything it could do.

My anxiety is not gone. It never will be. But I've learned to live with it. I know how to turn the volume of it down, to turn toward hard things to remind myself that I can do them, even dogless. There's no hiding at Tuff Girl. And that's not a threat. There's no yelling *at* at Tuff Girl either—only yelling *for*. It's the simple truth that Christa and her trainer-husband Mike and coaches, Karin and Hillary, leave you feeling a kind of inner power you don't want to keep hidden because it's like nothing you've felt before. There's no leaving your body while swinging a bell. There's being nothing *but* a body. I still float from time to time, but never as high up, and now I know how *not* to float. The same way Princess Hyacinth learns to hitch a ride back down on a friend's kite, I learned to grab a heavier bell.

While I wasn't looking, while I was simply showing up, I became a body I wanted to live in, even if it still sends me monsters most days. *I see you, monster,* I say. *I know who you are.* What a thing it is for my kids to watch me heave weighted balls at walls and climb a knotted rope to the roof like Spidey.

Remember her? I was starting to have someone to remember.

A woman who preferred to crush a few things before facing the remains of the day. A woman who sometimes forgave herself. A woman who didn't habitually bury anger. She, me: *I*. Nothing had changed on the other side of that door. I was the change now. My body was. As if it was the anti–Vegas, what happened at Tuff Girl *didn't* stay at Tuff Girl. What happened at Tuff Girl made everything else possible.

My walk to the car after was always the most hopeful part of my day. Whether the kids were fighting or not, my husband would get his packing done. Three a.m. was not the time to be thinking about *anything*. Planets can't just *do* that. I could still love dogs and not have to be one. I could love me and stop there.

One day, post-workout, I was sipping some water back outside the door that holds the stories, clearing my Tuff Girl bumper sticker of its seasonal mud and salt, remembering when my daughter asked me if Wonder Woman is real. I had told her that the one she saw in toy stores wasn't, but that I did know some real-life Wonder Women out there.

"Like Christa?" she'd asked.

"Like Christa," I'd said.

She'd gasped. So did I when it hit me that all these years later, I'd been given another Christa to believe in. Christa McAuliffe, the Wonder Woman of my childhood; Christa Doran, the Wonder Woman of my adulthood. Both now illuminating the powerful, haunting cosmos in which I'd loved and grown.

I started the car, drove toward whatever was next: tuff girl walking her tuff dogs, most likely.

"Get it," I heard Wonder Woman say.

Because of our busy road, the only option for walking the dogs without driving them somewhere is a .4-mile road directly across the street. It's a nice, quiet up-and-back once we've waited roadside for a clearing of safe crossing. A couple of other dogs and unknown quantity of wild animals frequent the little cut-through; plenty of smells for the taking.

As we crossed the street, the dogs startled at a raven's crass call. They're notorious mimics; I always wonder if the sounds they make that I don't recognize are the best evidence we have of mystical creatures, that ravens go where humans cannot, and so bring back only these unearthly recordings. Is this what a yeti sounds like? Bigfoot? Nessie? The great bird sat like a cake topper on the highest branch of one of the towering evergreens under which empty nips are scattered and squirrels spasm like they're on fire. We'd gotten this walk down to a science. I could have told you every spot they'd stop and sniff for the next .4 miles. The mailbox post at the brick house, the second shrub at the green house, the pile of leaves on the left side of the driveway at the serial killer's house (just an amateur theory), the tree roots at the wood chopper's house, the grass along the road by the duck pond, the grass at the edge of the brook, the pachysandra under the fish mailbox, and the pachysandra at the edge of the wooded area where the hill slopes up. I knew this because I walked the dogs every day, but I also knew this because while I walked the dogs, I thought a lot about . . . dogs. Out on the road in their company, I didn't miss a beat. It was the one place I still allowed myself to be one of them.

It's always felt curative, walking the dogs. Ever since middle school, when I took over the job of walking Agatha, I've felt many a problem solved in the quiet, steady transmissions through a leash. If having a child is like watching your heart walk around outside your body, then walking a dog is like walking your heart. In walking dogs, my heart endures. There is the satisfaction of offering them something so pleasurable to them, but it's also being witness to it, observing them from the inside out like a field scientist making rapt note of how a dog transcribes a road. Walking next to a dog, or in my case several feet behind one dog (Otter) and several feet in front of the other (Safari), I was reminded why I love photographs from the viewpoint behind subjects so much. (I take so many family photos that way, my friend Lauren finally commented, "I'm forgetting what you all look like!") I love letting my eyes wander through my children's bodies in the frame and fall upon where I imagine their eyes have gone. Walking a dog, I feel the same crush of souls. I may be holding the leashes, wielding my woman-made emblem of control, but I just feel lucky to be there. Otter and Safari darted back and forth over the craggy border where blacktop met grass the way I've seen old men vacuum the shoreline of Siesta Key, Florida, at the mercy of what's possible beneath their metal detectors. Otter stopped to sniff and so Safari did, too. Otter peed and Safari peed on top of Otter's pee. He always did, and this little act of seeming dominance by the nicest wolf always delighted me. We made our way slowly like this, hopping from one olfactory island to the next, the three of us more like a single, morphing creature than three individual beings.

I've weathered all kinds of trials and triumphs by walking dogs, including the dogless post-Agatha years of college, when my love of walking dogs led to an unexpected (and unwanted at the time) breakthrough in my equally ardent love of being the dog. I dog-sat for a couple of professors and a local couple, the

Warners, whom I'd put in their sixties at the time. Every March they headed to Florida for two weeks and I'd move into their house to care for their collie, Seiji. During the academic months, even when I wasn't caring for Seiji, they periodically invited me over for dinner, at which they always served breakfast—sausage and pancakes. While I didn't feel particularly close to them, they were kind enough, and a home-cooked meal was a novelty in my carless, small-town campus life, and I was not in the habit of saying no yet, so there I would sit between them, once again, the only child. Mom, Dad, me.

"How are your classes?" Mr. Warner would ask.

"Fine," I'd say. "I got into Jim Shepard's writing class."

"Do you want to be a writer?"

"Since forever."

"And squash? Has that started?"

"Yes. It's fine. We have our first match next weekend."

"Still with that same boyfriend of yours?"

"Yep. He's fine. He's back at water polo, taking all the classes I don't. He's premed."

"How are your parents?"

"Fine."

One night, he slammed down his fork.

"Is everything with you always fine?" he nearly yelled, shaking the sausage at the end of his fork at me.

I have no memory of what I said. I only remember feeling ashamed and mortified. My well-oiled tendency to please had finally failed me. This was the first time someone had so brazenly tried to crack through and name me. It was as if he'd never encountered someone like me before and was infuriated. I had certainly never encountered someone like *him*. Everyone around me had always been fine, too—and didn't want to hear if you *weren't*. Though were I to share my less-than-fine self in those days, it would never have been with him, he nevertheless shattered something in me that day—or chipped something, broke something old into a new beginning. At the time, I felt attacked, but he was actually giving me a gift. He was, albeit gruffly, building upon the practice Ina had begun teaching me years before, but with her gentler hand. *It's okay not to be okay.* It was permission. It was love—ornery love, but love. He wanted to know me and I still didn't know very well how to be known. I had no way of satisfying his desire.

I never went back to the Warners' for dinner. I took care of Seiji one more time, then got really busy again being fine—though with the new, unshakeable sense that something important had transpired, that amid the discomfort was something meaningful. It's painful to think back upon that young woman sitting so impenetrably at the dinner table, but in the pain there is the undeniable acknowledgment of movement, of a shifting internal biosphere. For the first time I was starting to feel what I was feeling. And in the long accomplishment of becoming, I was starting to wonder why I felt what I felt. Every now and then, I'd see the Warners at a football game or walking Seiji by the soccer fields. We'd wave. I'd walk over and give the dog a pat. It's funny to note all these years later that Seiji is the only dog I've ever known that I never felt connected to. He was aloof and neurotic. I could never find a way in. His discomfort made me uncomfortable. Or was that discomfort merely my own? After all, he was just being a dog, and dogs aren't always fine either. Dogs are adaptable and motivated but sensitive, too. Maybe Seiji was uncomfortable because I was uncomfortable. Maybe being my mirror was the dog's way of saying, It's okay not to be okay. And maybe because he saw me is why I felt a distance from him, too, and kept it that way.

Otter planted his feet and growled. There was a wheelbarrow where there hadn't been one yesterday. "It's okay," I told him. "It's a wheelbarrow." He wagged as we got closer and felt the okay of it, the way I also had to ease into new things post initial growl, trying hard now to be fine being fine and not fine. I walked him over to the wheelbarrow so he could sniff it, declare it harmless, the way my mom had once taken me to a birthday party early so that I could watch the man turn into a clown to make the clown less scary. Otter sniffed the wheelbarrow all over, his nose twitching back and forth and his wag widening. What an act of faith it is to listen to a dog, to be vulnerable, to feel your body learn from his, and, when a dog says he's had enough of the wheelbarrow, to believe him.

As the wheelbarrow and we parted ways, I thought of that thing people say about dogs (and children), that you end up with the dog (or child) you need most. Just like Jackson had taught me the most about my own emotional world, Otter had most boldly revealed in me my latest—and last—gasp at hiding in him. He wouldn't let me. He was the first dog I'd been unable to hide in. He was too dog. Right around the duck pond it hit me: he was the most dog dog I'd ever known. He felt more wolf than human, which explained why the back of his head smelled like smoke and woods. My other dogs had always felt far more human than wolf. I'd always been able to approach my other dogs as friends, peers even, but in order to best know my dog Otter, to be my best for him, I had to come out of my comfort zone and approach him as precisely what science says he is: a dog, a tamed wild animal in our midst. I felt a bit startled by this as we walked, Woman and Dog, down the road. He looked completely different to me than he had just one minute before. He wasn't Robin Williams or Steve Martin, he was 99.9 percent Canis lupus and it was nothing short of a miracle to be walking next to him, watching his hair ruffle from the muscles underneath, his nostril slits morphing like deep squids at the staggering particles of air I was too human to touch, to hear his jagged claws cleave the road next to my luxurious layers of socks and boots. At its starkest, the distance this revelation created between us reminded me of the foolish man and wise dog from Jack London's cautionary tale "To Build a Fire." As the pair heads into the Yukon on a dangerously frigid night, London writes, "There was no real bond between the dog and the man. The one was the slave of the other. The dog made no effort to indicate its fears to the man. It was not concerned with the well-being of the man. It was for its own sake that it looked toward the fire. But the man whistled, and spoke to it with the sound of the whip in his voice. So the dog started walking close to the man's heels and followed him along the trail." (Though my voice has never had the sound of whip in it, only belly rubs and treats.)

For once, I stood with a dog and felt as wholly in my body as the dog felt in his, the same way I felt when swinging a kettle-bell. It felt exhilarating, though with a strange side effect. As we walked back on the other side of the street, predictably stopping at the scarecrow, rock wall, sewer, I found myself fearing something I'd never feared before. *Dogs.* If Otter's wolfness made me feel better as human, then what was a dog to me now? The mere concept of a dog (essentially a wolf we'd negligently invited to supper) suddenly seemed bananas. Why on earth would we bring all these beasts into our home only to be eaten by them?

As we neared the corner where we cross back over to our house, I started experiencing this fear from the outside, as if from a me outside of me. I imagined bumping into someone on my walk and telling them exactly what was going through my head. I was even able to laugh a little at the absurdity of it—not that a fear of dogs is absurd. I think a degree of it is necessary to living amid them. When strangers ask if my dogs are friendly, I always say, "Yes, but they're also 99.9 percent wolves." Who are we to think we can predict the behavior of an animal even half the time? We can train them earnestly and behave for them, but they are animals nonetheless. What felt absurd was that anyone who knew me and my dependence on dogs would have found this whole development preposterous.

When I told Matt about the walk that day, about the dog fear and the presence of this outside Observer Me that almost made the whole thing funny, he told me what I was doing— what that Observer Me was doing for me—was inviting the fears in. *Letting the dogs in*, is how he put it. He told me that I'd moved from hiding within my fears to interacting with them, just like I had at Tuff Girl. This felt good. He is a doctor, after all.

Understanding better what Otter needed *and*, through his more complicated presence, what we as a family needed, I could get to the work of training all of us. *We could get to the work.* This made the whole situation less nerve-racking, more satisfying. I wasn't alone with it anymore, trying so hard to love Otter in a vacuum. *I wasn't alone.* Though I had been hoping it would be unmitigated love, it was Otter's complicated presence that brought our family together, as we surrounded the big pup who was essentially telling us that in order to live as a dog with ease, he needed more information and reassurance. The good news was, he was highly trainable, super treat-oriented, and driven to please. But if he wasn't getting clear signals, he got lost in the murk, and, as happens with any of us, the murk rendered him anxious and confused. It felt empowering to see all of this now, and to see such a clear path toward helping him. After all, Otter was the dog who in all of his ripe, rippling dog-ness had made me respect what a dog *is* more than any other dog before. Oh, I'd loved my dogs, I'd breathed my dogs, I'd done anything to make them happier, more comfortable, in every moment I could, but he's the one who pulled me closest to their specific nonhuman needs. He reminded me that he wasn't me in dog form but a beast, a once-wild animal living in my home. He demanded an entirely different relationship from me, and I was listening. Because of him, I try my best to approach dogs now as dogs, to give them their best dog life, not the best life that I, their human, want for them. It has undoubtedly necessitated a big mental shift, but it's one that feels welcome and relieving. It is a challenge to me and a necessity to them that I get it right. Dogs are now more than ever a subject of my curiosity, not mere fuzzy receptacles of my grief and heart, though Lord knows all they still carry. Like everyone I love, they tell me what I need to know. If I listen.

One of the sweetest routines that came about during this period was something Jackson called "Night-Night." When dinner was over and games had been played, we'd head upstairs for showers and bedtime. The dogs stayed downstairs for this—especially for "Talents," which we did most nights and sometimes involved a small karaoke microphone with rainbow lights that frazzled all over the walls and ceiling, sending Otter into a full-blown acid trip. Preferring to preserve his brain cells, we waited until the kids were squeaky clean and brushed and pajama-ed before Jackson called down the stairs, "Otter, wanna go Night-Night?" It didn't take long for his thick paws to hit the carpeted stairs. He'd arrive in Jackson's room, wagging from tongue to tail and smiling in the human way dogs smile. He'd either lie down on the floor by Jackson's bed or hoist three-quarters of his body up onto the bed in that way he seemed to think didn't fully count as being on the bed, just like the old "three on the floor" boarding school rule, requiring that when visitors of the opposite sex entered a dorm room, three feet must be on the floor at all times. Though in Otter's case, it was always "two on the floor." However Otter was situated, Jackson greeted him with some scratches, then read to him. I don't know who it helped more—the great big puppy looking for big love or the great big boy with big love to give. They'd both pass out and I'd click my tongue later in the night to wake Otter for a last pee before securing him in his crate. After all, I was learning that there's a time for dogs and a time when it's okay for those good dogs to go lie down.

The summer before, we'd left the dogs at home and driven with two other families to Keuka Lake. If it were just up to me, I'd bring the dogs everywhere, but I quickly fan out into a family of four and I've finally learned that, for the family of four, our vacations are better without them. Though Otter loved lake life and might well one day follow in the lake-leaping pawprints of Bookie, my husband would rather I stay longer in our cozy vacation beds than hop up and out the door for a walk and a feeding before everyone else is awake, and sometimes it's nice to feel wanted. It's nice to stay and say *okay*, meeting in the middle somewhere, standing on the sodden place where Earth meets a marriage, marriage meets its rooted stem. Last year, in the middle of the chaotic twelve-person scene, Otter ate a tray of mac 'n' cheese off the counter and vomited all night, so I can't say I wasn't also somewhat relieved.

Mercifully, we were not *entirely* dogless. Danielle and Chris brought their fourteen-year-old poodle mix, Lula, who was one-quarter the size of my big, fluffy pups and as sweet as the summer's seedless watermelons, which I can take or leave but Chris consumed like they were an essential food group.

It's a whole other thing, this life with a small dog, which I let myself settle back into for the first time since my Agatha days. I'd gotten so used to my heavy, heaving beasts, and the thrill of getting a big animal's permission to come up close, to breathe where they breathe, of watching my babies grow up under hairy legs and torsos that sometimes paused perfectly above them like tables.

But Lula could hop up into my lap, and I do love how a small dog can perch. She'd been their only dog now for two years, since their other dog, Mack, had to be put down after cancer crept up on and throughout his body. When the vet called to tell them the bad news, she'd shared something else they didn't know. Mack had had a bullet in him. The X-ray had revealed that sometime, somewhere, before he was theirs, that little Mack truck had been shot. Chris, who also has cancer in him—an incurable blood cancer called Waldenstrom's, a rare type of non-Hodgkin's lymphoma—is seasoned and stoic enough I wouldn't be surprised to learn he's also been carrying around an old bullet.

Lula spent the afternoon on the boat with us, testing the power of her paw pads as she neared the wet edge of the boat whenever Chris jumped in. Chris is Lula's person. She is a lover of all souls, but Chris is her North Star. Everything she sees seems to funnel through him. Danielle told me that when they first met her, she'd been living on the street for some time, scrapping her way through a dilapidated neighborhood. She feared men, so the big question was whether she would take to Chris or not. Danielle always laughs as she describes how immediately Lula took to him, like all that time she'd spent scrapping her way, she'd been scrapping her way to him.

That first night, as I was cleaning up the last of the kitchen, I caught sight of Chris's and Lula's feet next to each other on the bed in the guest room just off the kitchen, spooning like lovers, his hairless legs snug up next to her curly white ones. The sight of them there together like that—together wherever they were: on a couch, at the edge of a lake, on a bed—made me think about the dogs famously thought to be able to sniff out cancer, to insist in their language on malignancies where doctors have given the all-clear. Chris and Lula had met not long after his diagnosis, and I couldn't help but wonder if this little lamb of God could smell it on him in that first meeting, the one that was supposed to go so terribly but seemed ordained. I wondered if she knew and so had set up her tiny camp inside his cancer. His grace, too.

The next morning, Lula came on the boat with us. I watched Danielle and Lula watch Chris water-ski. That afternoon, we went to the waterfall, leaving Lula at home.

The path down the road that secretly leads to the 150-foot falls is largely a riverbed, which, depending on the season and weather, is very wet or very dry, but there are some dirt paths that skirt the crackled-slate-lined river where you can climb up and off-road. Jackson and Rae and Will and Alice and Fiona and Eliza were all off, the running kids, splashing through the shallows and, inevitably, purposefully, sinking themselves down into the freezing deep spots. We stopped and took pictures and waited for whoever at that moment was the slowest wing of the group.

There's a last little climb up and then there, all of a sudden, a waterfall spectacular enough to suggest we might have accidentally crossed over into another country, or life. We felt far from home.

There was lots of yelling, then everyone quieted, gravitating toward the large pool of water at the falls' base. They took turns standing under the hard weight of water falling down, having picked up big speed in so many feet of air. Alice found a bright orange newt and everyone gathered around her. Lizzy and Danielle moved to the base of a steep rock face while Chris and Ken and Matt wandered higher.

I can tell you exactly where everyone was and what they were doing because I was not part of the scene myself. I was standing in my shoes on the periphery, watching how marvelous life can be, feeling a little terrified. I cheerily waved to my family and friends, my eyes fixed on the rock cliffs, the craggled halo of sky carved out by so many years of water. *When is the last time those rocks fell? Are there earthquakes here?*

My husband waded my daughter into the water. They cheered. I cheered.

"Isn't this *amazing*, Rae Rae!?" I yelled, my amygdala quietly lighting on fire.

I checked the weather yesterday and it looked nice, but I didn't check today, and what about the surrounding areas because isn't that the thing about flash floods? You don't see them coming if it's pouring upriver?

This was not an unfamiliar feeling—standing on the periphery of joy, a bit joyless. But something felt different while I was silently panicking under the falls that day. I guess the modern Me would call it self-acceptance, but rather than wreck myself for it, I reconciled that on the periphery of this particular thing was simply where I felt better. I knew now to calmly let the dreaded scenario play out—to let the dogs in—to quietly lose everything, only to realize nothing had been lost today. The rocks were not only holding, they were blazing with life, rung with young trees leaning over to see us. My dogs were not *there* with me, but they were there with me, regardless, happening with me beneath the thick canopy of memories dotting and rotting the edge of the universe. Lula could still hop up onto her Chris, and Chris could still engulf her with his reason for being. I couldn't imagine I'd ever be without my tendency to burn stuff up, to see joy and immediately call up the ghosts. But, as Chris writes in "The Cancer Chair," an essay on suffering, "I believe the right response to reality is to bow down, and I believe the right response to reality is to scream." Doggedly, now, I will always do both.

Anyway, someone has to be the one with the camera and the snack bag and the dry towels, waiting to snug everyone up. Someone has to be the one who saw everything, who holds the story, who, like Safari, doesn't join them but sits where she is, happy to be alive and watching, happy to be who and where she is on the periphery, striking the beveled edge of where life gets made.

———

A month later, Danielle and I were floating in the minted wake of Higgins Lake when she said, "Maybe that's what makes a writer. So many stories to tell and all those generations of silence." She looked like a vintage movie star in her big-rimmed sunglasses and retro polka-dot suit, her hair twisted up at the back of her head.

We'd been talking about the generations of my family who'd been coming to this cottage for more than a century. Next to my childhood bedroom, it's the one spot in the world that knows me best. The hours I have sat at the end of our dock and done nothing but watched forged a kind of friendship between us. Nowhere else am I as mindful or still.

My grandparents Seaweed and Who Who (I named her that because that's what she used to say like a song to announce herself when she walked through the door) were also a great, big part of the draw there. Another incredible story of love and survival from the Greatest Generation, they were teenagers and engaged when my grandfather flew off to theater. He was the navigator on a B-24 Liberator in the Army Air Force. His plane was shot down over Hungary and, recovering from shrapnel wounds, he spent thirteen months at Stalag Luft III prison camp in Sagan, Germany. When he was finally liberated, he flew home to my waiting grandmother and they married five days later. That was the one thing he didn't seem to like to talk about, his time in the war—though he would answer any questions you asked. I've since wondered about that trauma, how it is said that the traumas a family endures can silently move down through generations like good teeth, alcoholism, and red hair. "When born you inherit what's burning," the poet Liam Rector writes. I've always wondered where that one went. Is there some trace of his trauma in mine? Why do I hope so? Why would that relieve me?

I had a particularly special bond with Seaweed, who was funny, curious, and a bit of an anomaly in my world. He loved to sit and talk in that way where you sit face-to-face, look each other in the eye, *listen*. He loved to know and to be known. When he asked me questions, he wanted to know my answers, not just something I thought he wanted to hear—he wanted to know *me*, even if it meant discovering someone different than he was. In fact, different with him often meant *better*. He loved a good debate and taught me how to disagree without ruining relationships.

"So, Chloe-Clump. How's Chester?" he would say as we sat in the swivel chairs by the lake. Chester is what he called anyone I was dating, no matter what their name was. (There never was a Chester.) He'd say, "When are you going to send me some writing so I can see how smart you are and how much you take after your handsome grandfather?" And, "Do you know how to play poker? You have to know how to play poker." Other times we'd sit up by the house under the great white pines that sometimes snapped during the bigger thunderstorms and he'd tell me everything he knew about chaos theory. He would always have a bowl with him. Inside it, either fresh cantaloupe or a giant, ripe peach that would inevitably drip all over the front of his shirt as he savored every bite while uttering the words "sheer poetry." He called the old-age bumps on his face his "smarts" and often credited "dumb luck" for his being here. He was a steady blue hole punched through a trembling white sky. His heart was mighty all right, but it was ailing.

He had two open-heart surgeries, the second in his mideighties, but that came with the risk of mental changes, which he developed, becoming increasingly agitated and paranoid. It was unbearable to me. I made a couple of trips to Chicago those last two years, but in truth, I was terrified of him—of who he'd become, of the whopping loss of him already.

I was six months pregnant with Jackson and in the cottage at Higgins when he died back in Chicago in his hospital bed. Who Who was with *us*, not him. We'd convinced her to leave him in the good care of the hospital, just for a long weekend. Some believe it was her leaving that allowed him to let go. They'd been married for sixty-four years, together even longer.

All of this I was telling Danielle as we floated and then sent our toes like mollusks into the clear sands. I told her that even though my world had always been full of beauty and movement and color and people and places and things, there'd been a kind of quiet to it all, like watching *The Wizard of Oz* with limited sound. Though they carried inside them the entire curled bird of my girl heart, the dogs were quiet, too. Conversations were often most notable for all that *wasn't* said—dead children and dead husbands and grieving and drinking and war all pushed up into a nearby tree for some other force to maneuver. Where does it all go? Deeper inside the dog body or farther out from the human one?

And so, I was bobbing there in the lake that raised me, telling Bobbing Danielle that I felt like I always wanted to talk more than the people around me, that I wanted to feel more, scream more, wild more. I wanted to be nothing if it didn't have wings. But I stayed quiet. I did what everybody else did. I did what everybody else said.

And that's when Bobbing Danielle said, "Maybe that's what

makes a writer. So many stories to tell and all those generations of silence."

I looked at my toes popping up out of the water again before the long, tapered snake of pines. I was too startled to speak. Because I felt like I'd been holding stories from the beginning. Too many stories to tell.

I wonder if the dogs feel this way. Is that why they sleep so many hours? Are they simply exhausted from all I've asked them to hold? Maybe what makes a writer also makes a dog—all the stories they silently hold, stories that could never make their way into a wolf. And how does a dog tell a story? Lacking context, there is nothing to withhold. Easy told me I was her sister by making space for me, by submissively slinking away; Agatha told me that a dog is a fine place to hide for a while by offering me her whole body; Booker told me he loved me by leaning on me; Safari tells me *thank you* by handing me his head; Otter tells me I've got work to do—that he, too, is relying on me to be human—by making no room in his barbarian body at all. A dog says what it means to say, while a human says things and means something else entirely.

I understand now that when my dad sends local weather forecasts relevant to the city I'm in, he's saying, *I love you—remember me.* When my mom calls from airplanes about to take off to tell me where the valuables are hidden, the extra-precious things, she's saying, *I love you—remember me.* When my dad brings me piles of magazines and newspaper clippings, having dog-eared all the pages that made him think of me, he's saying, *I know you.* When my mom walks into my disheveled, unvacuumed, midweek home and says, "Those pillows are *fabulous* on that chair!" she's saying, *I see you*. Knowing this—knowing how to listen in dog and human—is how I tell them I see them and know them and love them, remember them, too.

I hadn't been home to Brooklyn in almost a year when we boarded a train bound for the city for Thanksgiving. I am not alone in my complicated relationship with New York, both as a stand-alone city and as the particular city I grew up in. I didn't always feel like I belonged there and yet didn't know where I belonged. So, at least for my first three decades, lacking any other obvious answers, I often found my way back there. I lived in the city—in Brooklyn—for more than half of my forty-two years. I have many memories there beyond childhood. Like a cat, I have lived multiple lives within its gargantuan grip. But childhood has a more startling, permanent hold of the senses. Once inside the Big Apple, I cannot separate myself from my Little Me, or at least I've never been able to create the space in which to feel who I've become, and why—to know her. I know her in my life in my married home; I know her on the streets of New Haven and under the TRX rig at Tuff Girl; I know her walking the dogs through the woods. But something happens when I cross over the electric band of the city limits. There, my Little Me waits. She slips inside my shadow, and what it then contains is a strange amalgam of Me's, none whole, none thriving. I am everything I do and don't remember. I am little and big. I am quiet and loud; I am Easy and the Agathas and Booker and Safari and Otter all wound into a single thrumming nose. So it had been with a fragile trepidation I'd traveled there lately. It had been self-protective.

There was no telling what it would be now, with all my work in the dog and human worlds, hard-won.

Matt and I always sleep in my old room, which looks nothing like my old room anymore. "You are always welcome in our very beautiful guest room," my dad loves to tell me. Aside from some old books and the Top Shelf, there's hardly a trace of me left. The Axl Rose poster, glow-in-the-dark stars, and stuffed animals all retired long ago. Though two things are exactly the same: the old slatted wooden shutters and the patterns of light that sneak through them at night once the streetlight clicks on and cars pass through the city's best rendition of dark.

I lay in the twin bed that first night, unable to sleep. I was watching those old familiar patterns of light make their ghostly way across the ceiling. If I pushed the covers down, I was too cold; if I pulled them back up, I was too hot. This went on for hours as I turned from side to back to stomach to other side. Finally, I rolled onto my back again and opened my eyes to the world of my Little Me, happy and safe; frozen and afraid; full of the electric, yellow hope that tomorrow would be a better day, that tomorrow would never come, that tomorrow I would explode from the inside out, finally revealing the realest part of me. A shark swam through. Its big, wide head and long, white belly circled over me, a mysterious source of light from above—the moon, perhaps; the broken up bits of a ship's searchlight. Was it looking for me? There was Agatha warm on my leg. I lay still, gave up the will to sleep, watching the ceiling like I used to in the dark, the blank place against which everything hazardous and reverent always played.

Here's what you say about the teeth marks in the butter. You stand hard in your sturdy kid shoes and tell them Little Miss Tiny did it. You tell them she's thoughtless and naughty and doesn't care about anyone but herself. When they ask you, Who is Little Miss Tiny? you tell them exactly who she is—the tiny little girl who lives in your window seat. When they ask, How tiny? tell them the buttons on her dress are the size of mustard seeds. They'll love that. Then tell them about Brownie, the brown fur ball that lives with her. Talk about how nice and good he is so they don't think all their hard work was for naught. He's perfect. He has no eyes, no mouth, and he doesn't even shed. They will love that, too, because they love you, and you don't shed either. It was Little Miss Tiny who yelled all those bad words at the ponies you'd lined up for the pony show and squirted toothpaste in cursive all over the inside of your aunt's cosmetics case and told you that your dad wasn't late because of work but because there in the middle of the subway platform he'd caught fire, even though he had not, he was late because of work. But when you cut your own bangs, sweetie pie, say it was Easy the Afghan hound because she was their first baby and you were their last, if you don't count the one after you that died before it ever came out. Dead Sister Mustard Seed, or Dead Brother—nobody knows. Something the size of Little Miss Tiny's button. Little Miss Tiny is bad, but she can't be blamed for everything. They might stop believing you. And I don't mean, of course, that you should say that the dog cut your hair. Dogs can't use scissors! I mean, when they find the hair that has been cut off under your bedroom chair, tell them it's the dog's hair. It's not far off in color, and, you know, a forest of flying carpets could be made with that dog's long, blond tentacles, whatever a dog is. And the dog is many things, but the dog is not a liar. The dog is not a sister. The dog is not a kettlebell. Who are you, sweetie pie? Can you tell? Do gardens pop up when you look to the Earth with rage? Do ravishing linens fashion themselves from your grief? Best keep the shark that swims into your room at night, all the many terrible ways your parents have died, between us. Okay? Too messy otherwise. For now, look into their golden faces and see how much they love you. Feel the golden face of how much you love them. Your tears will go the way of the skunk body that rotted so quickly it was dust. You're still a squirt yet. You still have sex and lice and poetry ahead of you. Pull yourself together, Chloe-Clump. Say something else about Little Miss Tiny. Tell them her father lives in Florida. They like that, right? You know how I knew they would? They lived in Florida. You were born there. And what that means is they are now in the act of remembering, and memory is as good as love. They are leading Easy the Afghan puppy down the bloated, botanical streets of Coconut Grove. They are taking in the thick smell of plants bigger than your head. Let them. Because they are remembering you, Little Almost-Electra, and how you were hard to pull out into the rapturous city in which you were made. Three is the loneliest number. One is the number you know best. And there is only one you and you can't exactly say what a dog is yet, but the dog helps, the dog stays, the dog remembers you, the dog knows.

I was cold; I was hot.

The same thing happened the second night. The cold. The hot. For two days, I didn't sleep. And on the third night, my childhood room and my Little Me never came. I didn't need them anymore. A dog is what you make of it. Once my home, now they were my dogs. I let the dogs in and the rest was gone, leaving me to be *me*, there in my body, under the bone-white paint of a very beautiful guest room, indeed.

The Dog House

Lights out here in the Dog House. My last night alone with the wolves. Matt and the kids will be home tomorrow, and I'm wondering if they feel changed, too. Every time I take a trip, even for the weekend, I always feel a shift; some untouchable place inside me broadens in the leaving, or hops or shrinks. I went nowhere this week. Rather, I came home. I reckoned and reveled from within the bewitching, canined place where I live. And from where I sit on the screen porch, taking in the last light of my last night alone, I wonder how we will all come back together—if we will hum or blink or walk like horses, like first loves, like hearts that are much too broken or big. I wonder how they will return to me, holding their own versions of this week glowing within them like the stars the family of badgers holds to warm them through winter in the children's book my parents read to me at Christmas every year, those sweet round rodent faces, teeth out, tucked into their beds. There will undoubtedly be more freckles on them, like paw prints scattered across a heavily pollened car. I will tell them about the turkeys, who came back yesterday, pecking life back into the edge of the woods. *Our survival means your survival*, they were saying. And that I met the man from the accident. There he was this morning, standing near the brush where his car plowed in, staring. I wanted to ask him everything, I'll tell them. I wanted to know when his birthday is, what is his favorite color and kind of weather, if he's ever seen an owl midday, what that kind of survival feels like, and does he use a different voice to talk to dogs or just his regular one.

"I'm Jonathan," he said. He held out his hand.

I felt like I was shaking hands with my amygdala, I'll tell them. The counselor at their school, who talks about fears with the kids, not only teaches them about the amygdala, what and where it is, but brilliantly comes up with names for theirs. Cecil. Henrietta. Sharky. I'll tell them that I named mine Jonathan today.

On top of the sense I've made of my time as a human, the time with the dogs has been a radical gift. Safari is eleven, and though Otter is doing his rambunctious best to keep him young, there likely aren't a ton of years left with him. This is a fact my brain and heart process differently. I know it, just don't—can't possibly—believe it. His once-pink paw pads are gray and hard. His nose, which used to smell of hay, now smells of earth, death even. His eyes are rimmed with hairs of a sweet, hateful white. There is one glimmer of hope, though, a development the world unceremoniously writes for you. Otter and Safari have a new puppy buddy. Our friends Megan and Nick recently adopted a tan-and-white mutt they named Booker. He looks absolutely nothing like our Booker but carries the name beautifully, sweet, eager beast that he is. So when I think of the unthinkable loss Safari will one day be—the dog ghosts mounting like a love-wielding army—I also picture Otter and his own Booker together, climbing rocks in the forest, picking up sticks, licking life off the kids, the way Safari and our Booker did. That little line of dogs in my heart just keeps getting bigger.

In the dark, I lie on the floor with the dogs and tell them, *The humans are coming! The bright little humans! The Crotch is coming too!* (I swear it was the dogs who gave Matt this nickname.) They thump-wag against the floor and roll over at whatever the fuck I am saying.

Because I am human, I begin to worry. Because I am human, I let the dogs in. *What if they get into a car crash and die on the way home? What if I never hear their voices again? What if I die? What if they drive all the way home just to find me dead with the dogs in the Dog House? What if after this week, even though I am human, I can't live among humans anymore?*

These thoughts are not cumbersome. They come in and out like breathing, like kicking a ball back and forth with my kids. They bump themselves against my insides like house finches in a house. I open the door and they're out. My worries leave me to be whatever is left, whoever I am when I don't want to be the dog anymore.

I stay there with them for a while, miraculously feeling wholly *un*-dog. I'd thought this time in the Dog House would make me more dog than ever, but it's done the opposite. It's made me my most human. The same way you best portray loneliness in the middle of a crowd, it turns out you best portray humanness in the middle of dogs. I want to wrap myself in dogs, hold their heavy, wet muzzles in the rain, brush their coats, give them food and movement, tickle their barreled chimp chests while they sleep, but inside, I want to feel wholly human. I can love the human version of me, I can let the dogs just be dogs. I can let the dogs in until the fear *is* love. If I can see it as such, then it's just love, no matter what I am. When I am a bug, I want to be a slow bug, a fat summer bug that flies middle-high all the way through the forest. When I am a muscle—O magnificent muscles of mothers! When I am a dog, I want to be me.

I have a favorite picture of Booker. Well, I have a million favorite pictures of him. This one is from his last spring here—his last month, possibly. He's lying in our yard the way horses do, propped on his side. The grass beneath his long, black coat is very green, but the trees in the distant woods don't have their leaves yet, exposing a background of crackling tan. It's the kind of New England day when the sun feels stronger than it is simply because we've just survived the winter. Booker is soaking it in, his eyes nearly closed, his steady, terrestrial self leaning toward the light. His nose is lifted slightly to suggest all he's taking in with it. As close as dogs get to reflection, I'd say that's what he's doing here. He's making his shape in the elements, knowing, being known. He's doing what dogs do best, living out of every inch of his body.

I've only recently noticed something in the background. There, slightly out of focus, centered perfectly over his head, is the place where our grass meets the woods, the woven, sizzling spot where Booker died, and just beyond that, the spot where we buried him. The picture miraculously records his life *and* his death, the sun *and* the darkness. I visit this spot at the edge of the woods often. The kids and I sometimes bring rocks or leaves or flowers or dead bugs or birds or mice. I don't tell them that I have since buried a part of me with Booker—the vigilant, loyal little girl who was such a friend to me in my childhood, my Little Me who would not leave me alone. In order to heal, I had to let her go. *Thank you*, I told her. *I love you. But I don't need you anymore.* I laid her right beside Booker on the blanket. I shoveled earth, too, over her smooth, arrested eyes. I left them there together, together there they still lie—the little girl who didn't know how to help me and the great big dog who did. If a dog is love, you see, then Booker's death was just the beginning.

ACKNOWLEDGMENTS

You've heard about my dogs. Now, my humans (along with *their* dogs). This book would not have been possible without these extraordinary ones:

The poet Nancy White (Pete Seeger, Biscette, and Adam), whose zany, bighearted encouragement in high-school creative writing didn't only make me want to become a writer, it made me believe that it was possible. "To Chloe," she wrote in my copy of her collection *Sun, Moon, Salt*, published that year, "who's going to have to sign a book for *me* someday." Whenever in doubt, I read those words, and twenty-nine years later, I am here.

Karen and Jim Shepard (Birch and Audrey), who mentored me through my years at Williams College and life beyond in ways that have touched nearly every aspect of my being.

Amy Hempel (Savoy, Wannie, Morgan, and Gandhi), Sheila Kohler (Rambo), Betsy Cox, Martha Cooley (Bonnie), Rick Moody (Trouble), and Liam Rector, who filled my years at the Bennington Writing Seminars with wisdom and encouragement and so many luscious words I'd never heard before. Also,

Amy Gerstler (Gus and Bruno) and her gorgeous poem "The New Dog," which stopped me in my tracks the moment I heard her read it in Los Angeles more than two decades ago. It's *that* *poem*, the one I've carried ever since.

Eva, Janet, and John Irving (Dickens), who invited me in like family. John taught me about the athleticism of writing—the vital routine of practice, of showing up, of getting the job done. Also, that no matter how much they *look* like they might, wrestling dummies won't kill you in your sleep.

My agent, Meredith Kaffel Simonoff, who took me on three weeks after my daughter was born and has been with me through all the triumphs and turmoil of a full-time mom writing a book. Her humanity and wisdom are otherworldly yet somehow always translate this world for me. *What would Meredith do?* has become a mantra.

Bob Miller (Bella and Luna) at Flatiron Books, who had me at "Would you like to write a book about dogs?" This book was his idea. His faith in me seemed to come out of nowhere and is something I will carry with me for the rest of my life.

My editor, Lauren Bittrich (Clifford and Anne), who is not only a kindred dog soul but a brave and savvy reader. Her smarts, as my grandfather Seaweed would have called them, are as sweeping as her heart.

My entire incredible Flatiron team who've never stopped working on my behalf during a debilitating and devastating pandemic. Bethany Reis, Donna Noetzel (Duffy), Samantha Zukergood (Julie), Vincent Stanley (Fred and Harry), Keith Hayes (Sophie and Sebastian), Emily Walters (Stryker), and Chris Smith (Henry and Islay).

Julie Reinhart Balles (Pretinha, Kid, Udo, Buba, Leca, Woody,

Fofão, Faísca, Jade, Neguinha, Nick, and Ozzy) for her exquisite, tender rendering of our beautiful Booker on the cover.

Sudip Bose (Mischa) and the *American Scholar* for publishing the original essay "What Is a Dog?" and being so kind about it.

The Skadden Arps Operations Group (and all of their related paws), the greatest, craziest, funniest, full-of-heart work family I've ever had. Especially Randy Losapio (Champ and Grover) and his husband, Todd Doughty (Chip, Clancy, Muffy, and Lizza). Life is simply better with them in it.

My Bennington Writing Seminars loves—especially the brave and poetic Dinah Lenney (Sully), Sally Ashton (Duke, Sophie, Jeremy, and Maddie), and Sue Jackson Rodgers (Jake, Slick, Toby, and Finn), who taught me one decade before I needed this lesson how to be a mother *and* a writer at the same time—a feat that can best be described in this dog book as herding cats.

Lauren and Mark Greve (Bailey), Erin Scanlon-Oleskey (Moses, Tilley, and Ruby), and Dee Ginicola (Walden), for being Booker's (and our) people.

Kristina Nigro (Snickers, Jake, and Bailee), Ariana Shapiro (Tavi and Jackson), and Sara Ranson (Sandi, Sophia, Arya, Brutus, and Angie) for so tenderly caring for our various packs over the years (and for putting up with my inexhaustible instructions).

Heather Rife (Martha, Reggie, Sophie, and Kiko) for her brave knowledge of and respect for animals. It's not often a dog loves a vet the way Booker loved her; Lori Tomasko-Guliani (Pixie) for being there for Booker and us, too; Kim McClure Brinton (Maggie, Harriet, and Magnolia) for taking such incredible care of my sweet, senior Safari. I don't know how you all do what you do, but the world is so lucky you do it.

Christa and Mike Doran (Koa and Nova), Karin Christley (cats), and Hillary Smith (Daisy). *Tuff* only begins to describe these hearts and minds and bodies with whom I've been lucky enough to grow stronger, braver, and more present. *Grateful* only begins to define all I feel about them and my entire Tuff Girl community. I love you to the PR bell and back.

The divine and tuff Rachel Liu (Rhubarb) for her beautiful photographs, but even more, for her determined desire to see deeper than the glossy surface, to lovingly hold witness to whatever truth lies beneath.

Mental health professionals (and therapy dogs) everywhere, especially mine. This includes my Hairapist and friend, Keith Proto (Hugo and Cody).

All those brave and mighty souls devoting their lives to animal rescue, especially Pawtectors of Southington, Connecticut, and Companion Pet Rescue of Southbury, Connecticut. Thank you for saving Safari's and Otter's lives and for allowing us the easy work of loving them.

Harriet Ells (Jimmy, Buddy, and Stella), Whitten Morris (Shadow), Gerun Riley (Rudy and Phoebe), Katherine MacDonald (Tessie and Cleo), Kate Ramsdell (Bay and Grizzly), Cyd Oppenheimer (JJ, Archie, and Minnie), Matthew Swanson (Iggy and Dumbles), Kelly Berkson (Dexter), Beth and Kira Weinberger (Dusty and Ace), Emily Cleland (Ben and Jammy), Lizzy Donius and Ken McGill (Scout), Sarah Scott (Moxie), Cory Sells (Maizy), Aimee Meacham (Max), Angharad Davies (cat lady), Meg Andrews (Rusty and Molly), Michelle Bradford (Ivy Diana and Rusty Lewis), and Megan Craig (Booker) for the kind of friendships I've carried with me over bumps and books and miles. Thank you for your willingness to see me, love me, and so carry me with you, too.

Larry Levenson for his kind wisdom and for reminding me to say yes to life. Eileen Becker-Dunn (Mica, Sarah, Mozart, Shotzy, and Burt) and Lin Robinson (Wanda) for being such loving presences that fateful Halloween 2009 night—and always. Debra Boltas and Hanlyn Davies (Floss, Bete, Bounce, and Rajah) for so many lovely days of laughing, listening, futball, and friendship.

Danielle Chapman and Chris Wiman (Mack, Lula, and Rosie), whose love and guidance have brought a whole new language of gratitude and joy, and who, as my early readers, got (and kept) this whole ball rolling.

Dinny and Barney Shaw (Scram, Nifty, Bingo, Bourbon, Blue, Max, and Mickey), the mom and dad I was lucky enough to marry into. I've only known them fifteen years, yet it's impossible to remember life before their friendship, generosity, and love.

My cousins, Morley Vahey (Nikki and Deke), Anne Thomson (Nikki), Caitlin Sexton (Sheeba, Maggie, Bear, Bella, and Renfrow), Michael Thomson (Sheeba, Maggie, and Hunter), Dagny Lodowski (Beau, Calhoun, Snow, and Scout), Carolyn Martinez (Harper), Bethany Maneikis (Bella and Noodle). My brothers-in-law, David and Michael; my sister-in-law, Julie; my nephew, Cook; and my nieces, Lea and Kailyn (Rain). I am so lucky to have all of these sibling-people-away-from-home. We are spread far and wide, but family.

Speaking of family, I've been lucky enough to belong to many families, most formatively the Thomsons, Blands, Shaws, Ellses, Vases, and Feuersteins. At one time or another—but really, always—each has been a home to me.

My spectacular children, Jackson and Rae, who have taught me in the past eleven years more about myself than I learned in the first thirty-four. May they never stop listening and screaming, and may they always have dogs.

Their incredible teachers and caretakers—Michelle Munro, Linda Terrill (Arrow, Venus, Sparky, and Chauncey), Amber Morris (Macy and Lola), Susan Keegan (Clancy, Ditto, Rascal, and Chloe), Chester Sharp (Yara and Leia), Denise Quinn (Dash), Kim Yap (Travis, Luka, and Franklin), Felicia McKee (Hobo, Ziggy, Emma, Charlie, and Ladybug), Adam Solomon (Annie), Cassandra Spadory, Tracey Ruotolo (Cody), Cara Given (Bailey), Kossouth Bradford (Bruen, Shakespeare, Ozzie, Casper, and Taka), Rachelle Byron (Colin), Betty Peterson (Maggie and Tahini), and Dominique Ashby (Smash, Listo, and Maya)—who took extraordinary care of them during such crucial years.

My mom (Tarey) and dad (Bony), the first two loves of my life. They've given me so much that it takes my breath—and words—away. What an awfully brave thing to raise a writer. *Thank you. I love you.*

And, finally, my husband, Matt (Booker). I've heard it said that when one person in a house is writing a book then the whole house is writing a book, and in this house, with this book, that was undoubtedly true. Thanks to him for being the whole house with me, for bringing Booker that day, for promising to sit, to stay with me in the dark until I found the thing that was shiny: it was him; it was me; it was *us*.